from Calvary to Victory

Lenten

Reflections for

Individuals and

Groups

SUSAN K. WILLIAMS SMITH

UNITED CHURCH PRESS

CLEVELAND, OHIO

United Church Press, Cleveland, Ohio 44115
© 1999 by United Church Press

Printed in the United States of America on acid-free paper

04   03   02   01   00   99   5   4   3   2   1

Library of Congress Cataloging-in-Publication Data

Smith, Susan K. Williams, 1954–
    From Calvary to victory : Lenten reflections for individuals and groups /
Susan K. Williams Smith.
       p. cm.
    ISBN 0-8298-1359-4 (pbk. : alk. paper)
    1. Lent Meditations.   I. Title.
BV85.S63   1999
242'.34—dc21   99-34081
                                                    CIP

From Calvary to Victory

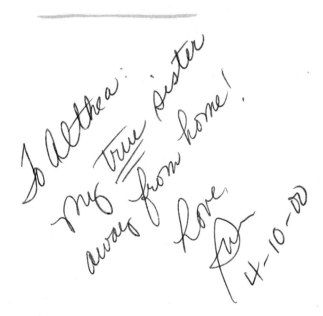

To Althea:
My true sister
away from home!

Love
[signature] 1X-10-00

This

*book is dedicated to
Mary Lee Kidd Simmons, and to
Caroline and Charlie Smith*

contents

acknowledgments

I first want to thank my mother, Mary Lee Simmons, now deceased, for always believing in me and for saying to her dying day that I should be a writer. I want to thank my children, Caroline and Charlie, for listening to me and *being quiet* as I banged away on the computer, and for reading the manuscript before I sent it out, giving me valuable input. To Kim Sadler, of United Church Press, *thank you* for being persistent and virtually making me write; and to Rev. Dr. Jeremiah Wright Jr., thank you for being my mentor and friend. Finally, to special friends Ida Edmondson, who teased me into writing and getting this in on time, and Jim White, for always seeing higher for me than I can for myself, I say thank you and I love you! To Rev. Barbara Allen of Trinity UCC, Chicago, my mother in the ministry, I love you for all that you've taught me. You were the first person to really teach me to "seek ye first the kingdom of God."

introduction

The Journey

O ne of the things I constantly teach is that it is one thing to *say* you are a Christian and quite another to actually *be* one. Saying you are a Christian is easy. *Being* a Christian is hard, constant work, probably the most difficult work we will ever do. Actually *doing* what Jesus asks of us, and truly being imitators of him, is no less difficult and takes no less discipline than does exercising every day or staying away from foods that make us gain weight. The whole goal of being a Christian is to be transformed from the inside out so that old things no longer have power and dominion in our lives; old "luggage" no longer has the power to weigh us down. Engaging in the practice of being a Christian, though difficult, is a liberating experience, and yet too many of us do not or cannot do it. Being a Christian means going on a journey to find one's Christ-self, to find out what the Word means by these words: "So if anyone is in Christ, there is a new creation: everything old has passed away; see, everything has become new!" (2 Cor. 5:17). It feels wonderful when the old has gone or is in the process of going! One would think that everyone would want it, and yet few of us really begin the journey, because we know the walk implies change. Let's face it: few of us are brave enough to do that.

I think of the recent and unfortunate predicament of President Clinton. It always appeared to me that God had the divine arms wrapped around him and that the president had a good relationship with God. Nevertheless, when there should have been evidence of a journey having been taken, a "change" having occurred, it seemed that the president kept God out as he admitted to the American public his sexual indiscretions with Monica Lewinsky. In his televised appearance where he admitted involvement with Ms. Lewinsky, there really was no contrition. Instead, anger and a sense of obligation seemed evident. A journey would have revealed a different man, a man directed not by his own thoughts but by the thoughts of God, and his attitude would have been far different.

When we confess Jesus and agree to be a part of him, we also agree to go on the journey. We agree to listen to and receive direction from One who has experienced the journey, not because he had to, but because he wanted to show us how to do it. We agree to go on this journey, not as punishment, but as the reward for confessing him. By walking this particular walk, we do not say that we are bad people; we are merely human beings trying to become more spiritual so that we can have a joy that the world did not give and the world cannot take away. Jesus desires for us to have real joy, real peace, real deliverance from our pasts and all the resultant victories that come from having those gifts. So, you see, the *opportunity* to go on the journey is God's gift to us. It is God's way of saying to us that there is a better way to feel while we are yet alive. It is God's way of showing us that the Christian walk takes us constantly toward *resurrection,* or new life, and that we are not doomed to suffer until we die, as many of us have been taught.

During this lenten season, I ask you to take a journey with me. I ask that you first identify a "cross" in your life from which you want to experience liberation and resurrection. What do you carry—and have been carrying a long time? Are there things in your closet that keep you in bondage and that you are afraid to reveal, even to God? Maybe it is a pain that will not go away. The pain could have come from something that happened in your childhood or something far more recent. It might be the memory of a moment you wished had never happened.

Maybe you are angry about something, and instead of being able to let go of it, you can still feel your whole spirit react when you think about the situation. Did your spouse cheat on you? Did a best friend betray you? Maybe your jealousy is the cross from which you need to get down this lenten season. Why are you so jealous, and what is it doing to your life? Do you feel empty or alone? Don't you want that feeling to go away so that you can experience the beauty of God's holiness? Whatever it is, name the cross that you have been carrying, and finally, this year, carry it somewhere and leave it there!

Doing this will require you to recognize how much you are willing to suffer, or let go of, in order to really experience Easter this year. Lent is about far more than giving up cigarettes or fried foods for forty days and then going back to the same old ways. Lent is about a journey, at the beginning of which you vow that once these forty days are up, "I will never turn back!" Being flippant about Lent and what it can mean for your spiritual health is like consenting to go through a major operation to have a cancerous tumor removed, having a successful surgery, and then deciding to get the tumor replanted in your body.

Lent is about journeying toward spiritual health and wholeness, never to turn back. It is about undergoing the scrutiny of a loving God who will excise the spiritual tumors that are blocking your joy and opportunity to truly experience life, the tumors that have warped your outlook on life and your relationships with loved ones. Going on a lenten journey is about saying to God, "I am serious about being your child and an heir of your realm," and in so doing, being given "ears that hear." It is about praying, as perhaps you have never prayed before, for new fruit in your spirit so that you bear witness to the Savior you say you honor.

So, Lent is not an easy experience. It should not be. Jesus' journey to the cross certainly was not easy. We are journeying toward a point of real pain—the crucifixion of a part of us that has been formed by and influenced by the world. We are journeying toward a place where part of the flesh that has defined us will be cast away forever, and as that familiar part of us is bled of its life, we will hurt. Change always hurts. But following the death of the old part, the "new creation" will emerge.

What do you need for this journey? First of all, you need to *trust* Jesus. You need to trust him that whatever you agree to give him during these forty days, he will treat gently. He will, of course, but you may not quite believe that God's way of handling your weaknesses is a lot kinder than the world's way. Trust in Jesus is essential for you to begin to let go and let him work on you.

Go back to the idea of the doctor who recognizes the cancerous tumor in your body. Just as you trust him or her to see the tumor and get it all out so that you can be healed, you have to trust Jesus to "see" the cancerous part of your spirit and get it all out. What is different between a physical excision and a spiritual excision is that you can *feel* the results of a physical excision more easily than you can a spiritual excision. The delay in feeling the results of your transformation can sometimes be frustrating and make you fall into thinking that nothing has happened. If, or as, you go on this journey, you have to make a covenant with God that you will not fall into that kind of thinking and that you will trust that God will do or is doing what you have prayed for.

The next thing you need on the journey is the *willingness* to open yourself honestly before God and allow a divine examination. We read in Psalm 139:

> *Search me, O God, and know my heart;*
> *test me and know my anxious thoughts.*
> *See if there is any offensive way in me,*
> *and lead me in the way everlasting.* (vv. 23–24, NIV)

It would be good to start this lenten season with that prayer.

To be willing to show your real "self" is not easy, not before people or God, because it requires a letting go of yourself and being vulnerable to correction. The word "correction" is used here because we are talking about letting go before God. If you were to do the same before people, there would be criticism—criticism, correction, call it what you will. But to be shown who you really are as opposed to what you want people to think about you is hard. Thank goodness, Lent is not about letting go before people!

At least in seeing you and showing you yourself, God does it with mercy, love, grace, and forgiveness. Human beings are less charitable. One of the reasons you are so reluctant to let go even before God is that you transfer the expected human reaction to the Divine.

It is not the same. Your being free is contingent upon knowing what you must be freed *from*. You have to be willing to open the doors to the closets, to expose the reasons why your insides are so messed up, and why you may be blocking the one Source who can pull you past it all.

It is hard at first. That is why I suggest praying the words of Psalm 139:23–24. Or we can pray together, "Here I am, God, at your feet. God, my soul looks up to you!" Whatever your comfort, find words that indicate to God that you are willing to let God into your life in a new way. By being willing to be open, you are also showing your willingness to change, which is, after all, the purpose of this journey. At the end of this trek, you should not be the same, which means that as you begin, you are not willing to be the same as you are right now.

This journey is a life-changing time for you. To change is to be repentant. You tell God that not only are you sorry for what God has to deal with on a daily basis, but that you are willing *not* to do it anymore. To change is also to show love for God. My ten-year-old son says to me all the time, "Mommy, I love you!" Of course, five minutes later he is doing something he is not supposed to do or not doing something he is supposed to do! That sort of thing was frustrating until I remembered the words, "If you love me, you will keep my commandments" (John 14:15). The light went on, and I began to say to him, "Yes, Charlie, I know you love me, but what does love mean?" Well, a big part of loving someone is knowing what he or she expects and being willing to do it! It means sometimes doing something when you absolutely do not want to do it, just because you know doing it will honor the person you say you love. We have to do that with God all the time. Few of us want to "turn the other cheek," for example, but out of love for God and for Jesus, we attempt to do it. Few of us want to "love our enemies," but again, because we love the Creator and the Savior, we agree to at least try to do that. It isn't easy; love isn't easy. But in "doing God's commandments," even the most difficult ones, we show that we love God more than we love the way we have always done things or would prefer to do them! So I remind Charlie of this all the time— with varying results. But for us to say to God, "I am willing to change because I am willing to finally love you," is a turning point in our lives, which is absolutely required on this trek.

The third thing you need on this journey is *discipline*. It takes discipline to "walk the walk." To rid yourself of something that is poisoning your spirit is difficult, though you would not like to think that way. Think of how hard it is for people to rid themselves of the physical poisons to which they are attached or addicted. How many smokers have been trying for a long time to let go of the habit? It takes discipline not to light up when everyone else is puffing away. Or how about those who are trying, and have been trying for a long time, to lose weight? Doesn't it take discipline to say no to the giant piece of chocolate cake? Or isn't it even harder not to sneak a cigarette or a piece of cake when nobody is looking?

Well, it is the same on this spiritual walk; only the reality is that Someone is always looking. If we go back to Psalm 139, we read these questions: "Where can I go from your Spirit? Where can I flee from your presence?" (v. 7, NIV). We must realize that we cannot flee. On this journey, you can make that fact your blessing or your burden—or both. God will not make you do anything during these forty days; the decision and the actions you take are all yours. God will yearn for you to be steadfast, however. If you stop smoking, you will improve your life expectancy. If you stop eating chocolate cake, you will stand to lose a significant amount of weight. So too if you are steadfast in cleaning your spirit, you will be free from the power that has been stealing your joy.

The result of going on this journey is that you ascend to greater spiritual heights. That is why you will feel free. Your "cross" will not necessarily disappear, but you will now feel the strength to be able to carry it—and know that this heavy journey is one with an end. You will feel the spiritual strength to keep moving, adjusting the burden, if you will, to allow you to finish the walk toward Calvary, but never getting to the point where you give up in frustration and stop moving toward your resurrection. You will realize that this cross is not your finality; it doesn't have the power to bury you.

As you continue to carry the cross with this new strength, a strange thing will happen: you will yearn for the prize! You will actually "hunger and thirst" for a newness in your life, based in large part on your perseverance! The words "Blessed are those who hunger and thirst for righteousness, for they will be filled" (Matt. 5:6, NIV) will become real to you, because you will *feel* that hunger and thirst! At the end of the forty days, if you are steadfast, you will have been emptied out of yourself and will be filled with the Spirit of God. You will be able to look back, and just as the funeral shroud of Jesus was found lying on the floor of his tomb, so the shroud that has covered you for so long will be gone. You will be one step closer to being what God has always intended for you to be: filled with the water that will never lose its ability to quench your desire for a closer walk and relationship with the Christ.

As we begin, I would like you to get something that will serve as a journal—a notebook or perhaps a diary—so that you can write down your thoughts, your struggles, your visions, victories, and seeming defeats. This writing will become as a prayer and will help you focus more on where you are and where you want to be. Every day, look at where you were the day before. Have you moved? If you haven't, can you figure out why? What praying do you have to do, what searching? The journal will help you keep track; it will become a very precious part of what you are attempting to do.

We are embarking on forty days of *deliberate, concentrated* work. We are walking toward Calvary, toward crucifixion, but we are also walking toward victory, toward resurrection. "So if anyone is in Christ, there is a new creation: everything old has passed away; see, everything has become new!" (2 Cor. 5:17). In the quest for newness, let us begin together.

one

Do You Want to Be Healed?

Nancy had been with Tony for a long time. Not forever, but three years is a long time to be with one person—totally committed.

The time had been tumultuous, to say the least. It seemed that even though Tony said he loved her as he had never loved anyone else, something was always wrong. She was always doing something wrong, and he was always mad at her. She did not understand.

She tried to change. He would criticize something about her, about what she wore or how she talked, anything, really. Assessing his opinions for herself, she decided his observations had some merit. So, she would work to change and think that maybe he would like her then, but somehow, it never happened.

She was afraid to talk with him honestly. If she shared her thoughts about something he was doing that offended her, he flew off the handle. She stopped trying. She carefully avoided saying anything to him that might set him off—and even at that, she was frequently caught in a maelstrom of name-calling or criticism. She was miserable.

His words to her and about her cut her to her core, and she shared with him how much it bothered her, but the pattern continued. And yet she loved him. He had been good for her in many ways. How many times had she, an independent woman with counseling clients of her own, told women that in similar situations, they simply had to decide to leave? But now the shoe was on the other foot, and she was finding it incredibly difficult to make a move. "Dear God," she prayed, "help me. I don't know what to do."

If you are going to get better, you have to want to get better.

Sometimes people get caught in a place of pain, physical or emotional or even spiritual. As a pastor, I have joked that I have not wanted to ask some people how they feel because once they start on their long list of complaints, they cannot stop! And by the time they finish telling me how bad they feel, I start to doubt how good *I* feel.

Often, I have walked away and wondered, "Do they want to be better?"

But in my life, there have been times when I have not made a real effort to be healed. I have been caught in a web of self-pity or righteous indignation or self-justification. I have blamed others for my situation, and in so doing, I have removed from myself the obligation of having to find a way to feel better. It is far more comfortable to point a finger at something or someone and say, "There! That's the reason (or he's/she's the reason) for my situation." Maybe this sounds familiar to you, too.

The hard reality is, what happens to us is largely because of us. As hard as it may be to admit, for example, many women who are battered are battered because they choose not to get out of the relationship. Granted, there are reasons, such as fear for one's life, fear of financial difficulty, and fear of being alone. A woman who stays in the relationship chooses not to press charges that might result in the batterer being put away. A big reason is fear of retribution. A bigger reason is her dependency on his presence in her life and her ability to find his "good points" in the midst of what he does to her. He beats her, she calls 9-1-1, the police pick him up, but she refuses to press charges. Then he gets out of jail, they have a "honeymoon" period where he manipulates her and her emotions once again, and something happens and she gets another beating.

Do you want to be healed?

Many of us miss experiencing financial prosperity or at least financial peace, not because of the world and its inherent unfairness, but because of what we do or do not do. You are in debt because you have chosen to be in debt. You are not compelled to have all the things you have acquired. You *wanted* them, and now you rob Peter but still cannot pay Paul. I admit that it is fun to spend money, but the bottom line is, people have money because they learned how to get it and how to keep it. How many times do we waste money by, say, buying a ninety-nine-cent cup of Pepsi (or a cup of ice with a drop of Pepsi), when we could have spent that same money and purchased a two-liter bottle? Or how many of us rent furniture, with exorbitant prices and interest, when it makes more sense to save that money and buy our own? I know. People make it hard for us to establish credit and to get the things we want, but our choices in response to life's difficulties get us into trouble and steal our financial freedom. Then as we pursue financial peace, we use the rent money to buy lottery tickets and then cry because we receive an eviction notice.

Do you want to be healed?

We do not get as far in life as we would like to go, not because of other people as much as because of weaknesses in our personalities. I prayed not long ago, "Dear God, please make me a good pastor, a good preacher, and a good mother." It occurred to me that part of my difficulty in my pastorate was not because of other people, but because of *me!* All my life, I have been an introvert. I do not have many friends, and I have been quite comfortable staying away from people, not talking or sharing or being involved. In my whole life, I never talked much on the phone, and whenever it even looked as if there was going to be confusion in a situation, I got out of the way. I even became impatient when I was in elementary school, playing softball, and the team would erupt into shouting about whose turn it was or whether something was an "out." My attitude was, "Let's play ball and leave all that noise alone!"

Although I am pegged as a relatively lively preacher, I do not come off as a relatively lively human being out of the pulpit. In fact, I have very little to say to anyone. Well, the people in the congregation did not understand that. They thought I was being rude or snobbish. I did not realize that, however. Once I prayed that prayer, God opened my eyes and took me to places I would never have gone by myself. All of a sudden, I could see what the people saw. I had chosen to be alone, so the people were leaving me alone. I knew who I was, but they did not know me at all. I had no idea how they perceived me, but after I prayed that prayer, I had to see my "ways" in their fullness and then be led by God in the direction that would begin to correct the situation. It was and has been painful, but I am a better pastor now because of the experience.

Do you want to be healed?

You want to lose weight, but you are definitely addicted to food—and not the good stuff, either. You are addicted to all the things that invite fat to knock on your door and enter. Fried chicken. Macaroni and cheese. Lasagna. Fettucine. Bread. Cookies, cakes, and pies. Fast foods, especially the French fries. And you wonder why you are gaining weight. When you are down, you eat. When you are angry, you eat. When you watch television, you eat. When you are anxious about something, you eat. When you are alone, you eat. And then you drink a diet Pepsi or Coke! Well, I guess the size ten will not fit anymore, but the weight gain is directly related to the choices you have made.

Do you want to be healed?

Nothing positive is going to happen to you on this journey, you will see no difference in the way you are now, unless you really want it. You have to want to be healed more than you want to hurt as you hurt right now. You have to take responsibility for yourself and for your actions, maybe in ways you have never done before. At the beginning of this lenten season, you have to say that you will no longer blame anyone or anything else for your situation. You have to say to God, "Show me my part in where I am today," and then brace yourself for the revelation. You will have what your spirit desires. If you want healing, your spirit will drive you to a place of healing, but if you do not want healing, your spirit will hear that message, regardless of what you say with your mouth, and you will stay right where you are.

The situation is well illustrated in John 5:1–15 (NIV). There was a pool called Bethesda at the Temple in Jerusalem, where a great number of disabled people went each year for healing. The story was that, periodically, angels would "trouble the water." When they did, the people would hurry into the pool, and some were healed.

Among them, says the Word, was a man who had been disabled for thirty-eight years. And on this day he sat, as he had for so many years, at the side of the healing pool, watching others get in and some come out healed.

I would assume that he whined because Jesus saw him and "learned that he had been in this condition for a long time" (v. 6). Perhaps the man explained that he had been sick for thirty-eight years and that he had been coming to the pool for healing for almost as many.

Looking at him, Jesus asked, "Do you want to get well?" (v. 6). And the man's answer portrays how so many of us act when we are in difficult or painful situations. We give up. We point a finger at others. We find all kinds of "reasons" why we stay where we have been for so long.

The man said to Jesus, "Sir, I have no one to help me into the pool when the water is stirred. While I am trying to get in, someone else goes down ahead of me" (v. 7). That is like saying, "Every time I try to get on my feet, someone knocks me down." It is part of life, but we do not often realize it. Instead of pressing on, we become professional or habitual victims.

Jesus looked around. The man did not realize that within him was the power to do whatever he wanted, with the help of God. He had to believe he would get better and want to get better more than he wanted to be disabled. When we decide we *want* something better, we frequently find a way to do it. And the first step is always turning to God and doing what God asks of us.

Jesus asked the man if he wanted to be healed, and my guess is that the man looked incredulously at him. "Of course!" That is what all of us would say—the women in abusive relationships, the families in the throes of economic hardship, the criminals being locked up again. *Of course I want to be healed!* Well, maybe—or maybe you did not realize you were quite comfortable being a victim until someone confronted you with yourself. I suppose that looking at the man's position by the side of the pool, Jesus could have said, "Well, if you want to be healed, roll over into the water and stop waiting for someone to do it for you!" The man was *so close* to his healing. Instead, Jesus said, "Get up! Pick up your mat and walk!" (v. 8). And at once, the man picked up his mat and walked, after being disabled for thirty-eight years.

On this journey, you must ask, *Do I want to be healed?* Or am I comfortable being where I am? Am I moving closer to my healing, Jesus the Christ, or am I stagnating in self-pity, fear, and victim security?

Do you want to be healed? Then get up and move toward God. Decide that this Good Friday experience has just about run its course.

Devotion Direction

Read John 5:1–15. Ask yourself:

1. On this journey, from what do I need to be freed?

2. Do I want to be healed?

3. Am I willing to put my hand in the hand of Jesus and do what Jesus says in order to be healed?

two

Letting Go of the Anger

She was so ashamed.

It had all happened so quickly. Sheila was in a good mood, thinking about the things she was going to accomplish that day when, out of nowhere, someone told her that a person she thought was her friend had lied to her. The lie was about something stupid, no less. And Sheila knew that she should not feel so bad. But it hit home; it hit a sore place in her over which she seemed to have no control. It was a place that hurt all the time, though Sheila was pretty good at ignoring it or at least denying it. When certain things happened, however, she would feel a surge of rage rise within her, and that was what she felt now.

Being angry was not really the problem; it was how she acted and reacted that made her ashamed. When she heard the awful lie, she reacted without thinking, called her friend, and blasted her. She could feel all of her pain, all of her poisons, rising up within her, but she had no power over the anger. And as soon as the phone call was over, Sheila knew that she had let her anger rule her again.

Where had it come from? Why was it able to seduce her, manipulate her, when she was trying so hard to conquer it? Too many times it had welled up in her and made her act wretchedly or say stupid, unkind things. For a while, she thought it was just part of her, but after making such a big fool of herself one day that she had no choice but to get on her knees and pray, she began to realize that the anger had deep roots.

She had rejected the thought at first. It had seemed foolish to her as she listened to other people talk about things that had happened in their childhoods that had lingering effects, but her spiritual searching made her realize that it was not so stupid after all. Sheila realized that who she was now was a composite of all the experiences she had accumulated up to that point. Some of those experiences had not been pleasant, and they had produced pain within her. Although she tried desperately to keep it well protected, it wormed through her at times and surfaced when she felt threatened or scared or rejected.

Sheila just wanted to be a good person, but when the anger rose, she acted in ways that shamed her and hurt others. She knew, too, that her behavior was not pleasing to God. Now, she had done it again. She had blown up, made a fool of herself, and hurt someone else. "I didn't have to react," she whispered to herself. "Dear God, help me."

At the end of these forty days, wouldn't it be great if you could say that you found the source of your anger? Wouldn't it be great if you could say that you risked opening yourself and your pain to God and found out that God is a healer after all?

Many of us say that we do not see miracles today, and we are disappointed that God did so many in biblical times but does not seem to do them today. You must understand that in order to see a miracle, you must *expect* a miracle to happen. And certainly, getting rid of anger that has been within you for years, rotting your spirit and your soul, would be a miracle.

Where did your anger come from? Have you ever risked asking yourself the question or sat still long enough to hear the answer? Or have you consistently denied that you have a problem? No? Well, it is not normal to fly off the handle. It is not normal to get mad over little things. It is not normal to blow things out of proportion or to see the absolute worst in situations. "Those of steadfast mind you keep in peace—in peace because they trust you" (Isa. 26:3). But the sad fact is, too many of us do not trust God enough to give God our spirits and all that our spirits contain, so we miss out on the miracle of peace on earth.

People become angry, or are angry, for a lot of reasons. You might be angry because when you were a little girl, you were molested by someone you loved and trusted. You are angry at him, and you are perhaps angry at your mother for not believing you when you finally told her.

Perhaps you are an African American, and as you think of how this country has denied you your "inalienable rights," you get angry. You get angry at the fact that slavery existed and demoralized your race, and that justice still seems so elusive, but nobody seems to care.

You are a Native American who feels the sting of having been denied the respect due your people. You hate it that Native Americans are still basically ignored, and that civilized people feel no outrage about your people being ignored or relegated to live on reservations.

You are angry because you feel that the government has been too invasive, that in your opinion, it has listened to everyone's cry but your own. You feel the anger rise as the federal government interferes with the way this country was meant to be run.

Or your rage surges within you as people you feel are too liberal refuse to see that abortion is wrong. It is outright murder, and the only way it seems you can get attention is to do something or say something drastic.

The source of your anger might be like something that has just been described, or it might be far more personal in nature. You still sting at the memory of those who used to call you names, tease and taunt you mercilessly, because you were overweight growing up or too plain. You remember how hard you tried to fit in, but how they kept you away. You especially remember the ringleader of the group that rejected you, and the memory can still bring tears to your eyes. Or you are angry because your mother was not a mother to you; she was an alcoholic and was mean to you and your siblings, or she was more concerned with having a man than with being a mother. Either your father was not at home, or he was abusive physically, verbally, and emotionally to all of you when he was there. And you are expected to have a successful relationship today?

The anger is there.

So, I ask again, where did *your* anger come from? What sets you off, and why? Several years ago, the women at my church began a prayer circle, where we dared risk giving our souls to God. We covenanted with God that we would be honest, that we would open up to God for the purpose of healing. We agreed that we would trust God, and we actually asked God to break us. It was risky, but as we met and prayed, we realized that all of us had things in us that were blocking a more perfect union with God's Spirit.

For a while things went pretty smoothly; we talked, shared, and sought security as we felt some of our defenses being methodically chipped away by the Holy Spirit. But then, we had an all-night prayer vigil, and it was miraculous the way, all of a sudden, it seemed that God came and stripped us down to our cores. At the all-night prayer vigil I realized that my biggest pain, the pain that translates most quickly into anger, is that of rejection. God revealed to me how the reality of rejection is too much for me to bear, and the fear of rejection drives my actions and reactions.

It happened not only to me, but also to all the other women that night. It was like Pentecost all over again, only this time in a twentieth-century church. As I opened my tear-filled eyes, I could see the women lying on the floor, sitting in the pews, kneeling at the altar, crying, yet seeming so free. Oh, the revelation hurt, and yet it was somehow liberating! My anger came from my pain of having been without my mother and feeling rejection, which made me afraid of rejection.

I had felt rejection. As a small child, I had lived with foster parents as my mother worked—I do not know where. I just remember her coming to see me on some weekends. I remember not feeling really like a part of my foster families, though they were nice enough to me. I remember my mother telling me that my birth father did not want me. I remember these things, and as I went through that night at the church, I remembered more.

I remembered how, when my mother married my stepfather, his family did not really like me or accept me (or at least that was how I felt). I remembered feeling that they were all so beautiful, and I was not. I remembered how my new cousins would laugh at me and point and call me "Eskimo eyes" or "Chinese girl," and how I began to feel very lonely. I remembered how I slowly retreated into myself and began to find solace and comfort with myself.

I remembered how in school I kept to myself. People liked me well enough, but I never trusted others enough to reach out to them. I was alone by choice because it felt safe. I hated being rejected by my stepdad's family. I hated feeling like an outsider. And so I made myself what I hated—an outsider.

My pain and fear of rejection began to form a seed of anger within me, and my choice was to go inside myself and stay alone. I realized that I carefully protect that part of myself, but whenever I feel rejection, the anger comes out. Mostly, I am quiet, but when it gets to the point that I cannot contain it, I blow up. I yell. I scream. I act before I think.

Does that sound familiar? Isn't that what happens to you in some way or another? Isn't that what we have seen happen to young high-school kids who have been unable to handle their pain at being rejected, and they have completely lost control, to the point of killing innocent people?

Anger is a dangerous, toxic emotion for us to carry around, and it interferes with our spiritual maturity. It keeps us from being peacemakers—that is, having peace within ourselves and therefore being in a state of readiness to be connected to God. From the Bible we learn that anger makes us do foolish things (Prov. 14:17). The psalmist said, "Refrain from anger and turn from wrath; do not fret; it only leads to evil" (Ps. 37:8, NIV). And James urged, "Be quick to listen, slow to speak and slow to become angry" (1:19, NIV). Easier said than done, though. The truth is, if we do not recognize that we must identify the source of our anger, it will always have control over us and lead us to do things, say things, and think things that interfere with our well-being.

Saul knew about anger. At one time a glorious and respected ruler of God's people, Saul had a weakness, as we all do. Like too many of us, he did not try to identify its source.

Things were okay until David came along. Saul liked David at first. The young lad was smart, industrious, and eager to please Saul; he was like a second son. Saul loved David "as himself" (1 Sam. 18:1, NIV). Saul loved David so much that he kept the young boy with him and would not let him return to his father's house. Saul wanted to train him and develop him and take the credit for it!

The Word says that "whatever Saul sent [David] to do, David did it so successfully that Saul gave him a high rank in the military" (1 Sam. 18:5, NIV). The mentor was satisfied that his protégé was doing so well.

Then David did a little too well. We do not know how Saul grew up, what memories he had, what things in life he was trying to deny or forget as he forged ahead. But Saul was a human being with baggage, as are we all, and no matter how we try to forget where we've been and what we've experienced, invariably our pasts and the baggage we bring from those pasts affect our present. Saul was no different. There was a part of him that loved David and wanted him to do well, even taught him so that he *would* do well. But something inside Saul was ignited as David did too well, better than Saul, it seemed to him, and received more praise. Saul didn't want to feel this . . . jealousy, this insecurity, that made his cheeks hot and made something happen to the very organs in his body! *He didn't want to feel it!* But it was there, and it had an effect on him and *control over him.* The Word says that "whatever Saul sent David to do, he did it successfully" (1 Sam. 18:5). For a healthy spirit, this would have been a compliment.

But as David received more and more accolades, Saul's cross began to weigh him down. "Saul was very angry; . . . and from that time on, Saul kept a jealous eye on David" (1 Sam. 18:8–9). Saul's life, and all that had produced his personality, was now intruding on his present and destroying for him what could have been a glorious moment!

It all came to a head when as David and the men were returning from a battle with the Philistines, the women came out to greet the warriors "with singing and dancing." They oohed and aahed over the men and sang boldly, "Saul has slain his thousands, and David his tens of thousands" (1 Sam. 18:6–7, NIV). It was a day of celebration and joy for everybody except Saul.

His spirit, seduced by envy, began to boil. Why was he envious? Did he not get enough praise when he was growing up? Was he always being compared to someone, maybe an older brother? Was his dad always expecting more of him than he could produce, making him feel frustrated and jealous when his father seemed proud of the accomplishments of someone else?

What was it? We do not know that Saul ever asked that question, but it is clear that his pain, his hurt, ruled him, and it reared its ugly head as the people praised David. Saul heard the comparison between himself and his student, not the unspoken praise of the teacher. And the Word says, "Saul was very angry; this refrain galled him" (1 Sam. 18:8, NIV). He could not believe it. He had been ruler all that time, winning hundreds of battles, and David went out one time, had a lucky day, and the people forgot! Saul ached with the pain of envy. He began to believe that David was against him and would soon be after his kingdom.

What happened? "The next day, an evil spirit from God came forcefully upon Saul" (1 Sam. 18:10, NIV). From God? An evil spirit from God? Could that be? It does not mean that God sent evil to Saul; the evil existed within Saul's spirit already. It does mean that Saul's pain produced a toxic spiritual environment that made him act in ways displeasing to God. God could not help because *Saul had not recognized or confessed his pain.*

What was his pain? Was he afraid of rejection? Was he afraid of not being liked? Was he insecure about himself, and that was why he was unable to share his success? Were the adulating words of the women toward David a reminder of a criticizing parent, one for whom he could never measure up? We do not know, but it is probable that if asked, Saul would have denied he had a problem. It is likely that he would have said David was the problem and he was simply acting or reacting as any sane person would in the same circumstance.

Maybe. But those of us who call ourselves Christian are called to something higher. More important, we are allowed to enter a healing chamber that is like no other if we simply acknowledge that we have a need for that healing. Being angry like that is a spiritual illness, and like a physical illness, it cannot be treated unless it is acknowledged. Saul could have been healed. He could have been transformed; God could have revealed, first, his pain, second, the source of that pain, and third, a way for him to release and be freed of that pain. Because he did not give that feeling to God and he continued to act upon raw emotion, Saul ended up losing his blessing, his respect in the community, and ultimately, his life.

Is that where you want to go? Is that how you want to end up? Don't you want to know how it feels to have a divine healing, to be able to explain what used to be inside you, but that God took out? Whatever has had you angry for so long is not worth the price you are paying—which is not having peace of mind. Our days on earth are numbered. Do you really want to waste them being angry?

During these forty days, you are to search, open yourself up, risk revelation, and seek liberation. Your cross is heavy; I can feel it. And yet it is not too heavy for God to lift. You just have to ask God to help you.

Devotion Direction

1. Read 1 Samuel 18–19. Ask yourself:

a) Am I like Saul? Do I have anger in me that is making me do things I hate?

b) What is its source?

c) Do I trust Jesus enough to give my anger to him?

2. List the last several times you were angry. What were the motivating circumstances?

3. Confess those times if you have not already.

4. Every day, write down the times you felt your anger about to well up in you, and record how you handled it. Are you seeing a pattern of letting go and letting God?

three

An Unforgiving Spirit

It had never been easy for them as children. Mother was alone and had to work long, hard hours in an unskilled job to support them.

There were just three of them—three girls. They all knew their father. He lived close by, and sometimes they would see him. But he never acknowledged them. He acted as if he did not know them. Even when Katie, the youngest one, would see him and yell out, "Hi, Daddy!" he would ignore her or only nod slightly.

Their father's treatment of them bothered them all, but especially the oldest girl, Lela. She could remember when he had been around, yelling at her mother, coming home late, not seeming to care, even then. She could remember when she wanted him to come to one of her school events, and he promised he would. But he never showed up and never apologized about it. Then there was the time when he said "no" straight out when she asked him if he would come to school and hear her play in the orchestra concert. She had been so hurt; she could still remember the sting of her hot, angry tears on her face. She could also remember deciding that she would never forgive him.

As time passed, he gave her more and more reasons why she should not forgive him. There was the time when Mama was sick, and he would not take her to the hospital. She had to take a taxi.

Then there was the time when Leslie, the middle child, had given him a certain aftershave for his birthday. When he saw it, he pushed it away angrily and said, "I don't even like that fragrance!" Leslie was wounded, but Lela grew more angry and unforgiving.

Then one day, he did not come home at all—or the next day or the next. Mama was frantic. Had something happened to him? And then one day, when Lela came home, Mama was crying her eyes out. It seemed that Daddy had found a new person in his life and was living with her. He was leaving the family and was going to marry this new lady.

Lela fumed. That was the last straw. Her mother could see her fury and said to her, "Lela, we have to forgive him. He'll realize one day what he's done." Lela stiffened. "I think he should burn in hell!" It was only because her mother was in such pain that she could have said such a thing and gotten away with it, but even today, Lela could remember her mother saying, tears in her eyes, that it was for God to give out the punishment if there was any to be given, not us.

That had made Lela even angrier and more resolved in her intention never to forgive him. She was angry that God could even allow God's children to go through such an experience and angry that God would not allow God's children to do something to "get back" at others who hurt them. From that day forward, her heart was closed—to God, to her father, and though she did not realize it, to many men. There was no trust, no love, or no room for anything but hatred and resentment.

The girls grew up. They had their own families and moved away from the small town in which they grew up. One day, Lela got a phone call from Leslie. "Lela, Katie and I have been talking. We think we should take our children to meet Daddy. We might be mad at him, but they don't know him and it doesn't seem fair to keep them from him. Do you want to join us?"

At that instant, Lela felt her whole being tighten up. The audacity of their even asking her! Didn't they remember? Hadn't they recalled how miserable their mother was all their lives? And now, they wanted to make some sort of amends?

"I can't believe you're asking me that," Lela said coldly. "No, I won't be joining you."

Leslie protested, "But, Lela, maybe he's changed. He's our only father—"

Lela cut her off. "He's not my father, and I'll be darned if I let him near me or my family! *No!* I won't be joining you!"

Katie and Leslie made the trip without their older sister, and despite some early difficulty and adjustments, the visit went well. It seemed that their father did have some remorse and was genuinely glad to see his children. And he loved his grandchildren. The family began to make the difficult trek forward to a place of absolution and peace.

The time was cut short, however. Not long after the visits began (they visited him three summers in a row), Katie got a call from her stepmother. "Katie, your dad is sick, really sick, and he's asking for you . . . all of you."

Katie could feel her stomach tighten up, and she was really surprised that she felt anything for him like that. She did, though, and quickly called her sisters. Leslie said she would be on the next plane, but the call to Lela went quite a bit differently.

"What do you want me to do about it?" Lela asked coldly when Katie told her about their father. "So, he's sick."

Katie paused. "But he might die, Lela. Don't you want to even try to make peace?"

Lela could not stop the swell of hot, angry tears. "I don't care about him. He never cared about us. Why should I care about him, even now? A long time ago, I said I hoped he burned in hell. Well, I still hope he does. I hope he suffers. I hope as he dies, he remembers how he treated us, how he treated Mama. No, I won't be going. Don't call me about it again." And Lela hung up the phone.

Two weeks later, along with a lot of friends and people their father had known, only Katie and Leslie stood at the graveside of their father. Lela was not there.

An unforgiving spirit is as toxic to your being as a toxic environment is to your body. Just as poisonous fumes from the environment can invade your physical body and eat away at healthy cells, unbeknownst to you, poisonous vapors from your spirit can eat away at the fiber of your being.

You are on tranquilizers and antidepressants. Why? Because something has eaten away at your resolve, your resilience, your very spirit. Unfortunately, though you do not realize it, those external agents are not going to be able to help you in the way you need to be helped.

Why can't you forgive your mother? Your father? Your former spouse? Or someone else? Why, after all these years, are you still as caught up in your pain as you were when the incident happened?

Things happen. It is a part of life. We learn from our mistakes. For the most part, we do not really mean to do some of the things we do (although some of us do!). We are not as aware at certain points in our lives as we are at others of how devastating our actions can be to others. We may not be sensitive enough or mature enough to care. We live for the moment and forget that there are consequences to our actions.

And so we make blunders—say things, do things, participate in things—that will only hurt others and, ultimately, us. That is what happened to you. Someone was too inexperienced, too selfish, too self-centered, too immature, to be able to concentrate or care about how you would have felt when "the incident" happened. But people change. Haven't you?

Anger gives us an unforgiving spirit. I remember when I was divorced from my children's father. I was angry and hurt, and I think I probably vowed that I would never forgive him. Well, the children visited him every other weekend, and he always brought them to church. To his credit, he never stopped doing that. After the service, he came to church to take them back to his house for the rest of his visit. As I would see him walking up the walk to the door of the church, my blood would boil, my spirit would recoil, and I could feel all that anger, all that pain. It was the dead of winter, and I, the pastor, would tell the deacons, "Don't let him in this church." Mind you, we were not in sunny California. We were in Columbus, Ohio, in winter, when the temperature was frequently in the twenties. And yet my unforgiving spirit would not let me go.

One day, I could hear the Holy Spirit say, "Let go!" I was angry and said, "No! He hurt me and he has to pay." The blessed Holy Spirit said again, "Let go! My peace is sufficient for you." I could feel my face flush, the tears brimming in my eyes. "I can't," I whispered. "You don't understand how much he hurt me." And the Holy Spirit said to me, "Don't you realize how you've hurt *me*? And hurt others? Let it go, Susan."

And so, moving completely by and with the power of the Holy Spirit, I went to the door that winter Sunday morning, and when my ex-husband came to the door, I personally opened the door and said, "Why don't you come in?" Everybody was shocked—my ex-husband, the deacons, the members who knew of my actions, and me. It was as if I was standing on the side, watching the Holy Spirit work.

My ex-husband paused. I said, "Oh, come in. We're having dinner this afternoon, and I'm sure the children would love for you to eat with them." He entered the building, and I took him to the children. I made sure he got something to eat. Then I went into my office, amazed at how *free* I felt.

Oh, all the pain was not gone, but the hold that the unforgiving spirit had on me had been loosened. The powers and principalities that had ruled my being were being replaced by God's angels, which wanted me to experience spiritual freedom and growth. I repeat, the pain was not gone; I could still put my finger on it. But I was no longer bound by an unforgiving spirit, and I could begin the process I needed to go through in order to purge it from my being.

It is a necessary part of being alive—getting rid of an unforgiving spirit. Its presence is a constant reminder that we have not "let go and let God." It is extremely difficult to let go, because holding on to it gives us a false sense of security and maybe power. It makes us think that we have a shield up against being hurt again—and it does keep the hurt away to an extent—but the same shield also keeps away the blessings that God sends our way. When we hold on to an unforgiving spirit, we box in all the toxins of the spirit that kill us and cause physical and spiritual disease, and we block out the fruit of the Spirit—love, joy, peace, patience, kindness, goodness, faithfulness, gentleness, and self-control (Gal. 5:22–23). God wants us to bear the fruit as evidence of our being connected to the Divine Self, but we absolutely cannot if the toxins are running rampant. And an unforgiving spirit is definitely one of those toxins.

It is a journey to let go of an unforgiving spirit. Too many of us carry the cross of an unforgiving spirit, but we have to realize that we do not have to carry it. We do not have to believe that the only way we will feel better is to hurt the person or persons who hurt us. That belief is false. The truth of the matter is, they most likely do not have a clue about how badly we were hurting in the first place, so all that energy we waste in trying to make them hurt is just that—wasted.

But there is a larger, looming reason why we are bound to release an unforgiving spirit: we experience forgiveness every day. God forgives us every day for the things we do and the things we fail to do. Grace is freely given to everyone: God gives the same amount of grace to the murderer as to the churchgoer; the late Governor George Wallace, once he repented, got as much grace as did the Rev. Dr. Martin Luther King; if Jeffrey Dahmer repented, he received as much grace as did Mother Teresa. God has an open ear and is ready to forgive us if we ask. As Christians, we are bound to try to imitate Jesus, who is God incarnate ("Be imitators of God, therefore, and live a life of love, just as Christ loved us and gave himself up for us as a fragrant offering and sacrifice to God" [Eph. 5:1–2, NIV]). Realizing all of that, we have no choice but to let go of an unforgiving spirit.

At the last day, who knows who might be sitting next to you? It might be Eleanor Roosevelt, Ruby Bridges, Justice Thurgood Marshall, President John Kennedy, your mother, or your sister. Or it might be Jeffrey Dahmer, Senator Joseph McCarthy, Adolf Hitler, or Willie Horton. Grace and forgiveness are freely given to those who repent; confession and belief in the Sovereign Jesus are the only things required for salvation (Rom. 10:9). Now, what are you going to do?

Do you remember the story of the unmerciful servant found in Matthew 18:21–35 (NIV)? The story begins with Peter asking Jesus, "Lord, how many times shall I forgive my brother when he sins against me? Up to seven times?" Even that amount seems excessive for those of us harboring an unforgiving spirit. Seven times? That is enough. But Jesus, in his customary unsettling manner, answered, "I tell you, not seven times, but seventy times seven." I know, I know, he was talking about spiritual perfection almost; it is no accident that he used the numbers seven and seventy. The numbers denote perfection, but Jesus has no qualms asking us to abide in that way because we are supposed to imitate him.

So then he told the story. There was a king who wanted to settle accounts with his servants. As he began the settlement, a man who owed him ten thousand talents was brought to him. Since he was unable to pay, the master ordered that the man and his wife and his children and all that he had were to be sold to repay the debt. It was legal to do that back then.

The servant fell to his knees before the king. "Be patient with me," he begged, "and I will pay back everything." The servant's master had mercy on him—demonstrated a forgiving spirit—and let him go.

But when the same fellow was released, he saw someone who owed him far less than he owed his master. Remember, the man's life, his family, and his possessions had just been spared by one who had a forgiving spirit. But the man forgot, and when he saw the person who owed *him,* he demanded full and immediate payment.

The man could not pay, and though he asked for mercy and forgiveness, the forgiven man refused to listen and had the man thrown into prison until the debt was paid. Do you see how an unforgiving spirit will lead you to do foolish, unkind things?

Observers of the scenario had recently seen the man being forgiven, and they were aghast. They went to the man's master and told him what had happened. The master was livid. "This is the kind of thanks I get for forgiving you?" he thundered. In disgust, he bound the man over to jailers to be tortured until the debt was paid.

And that, Jesus said, is how our heavenly Parent will deal with us unless we forgive our brothers and sisters.

Now, some skeptics might be saying, "Oh, no. God won't torture me if I don't forgive." No? Well, isn't it torture to live without peace of mind? And isn't it torture to always have a feeling of unfulfillment? And couldn't it be torture to get to your last day and wonder, too late, whether your unforgiving spirit was going to cause you trouble?

Let it go. *Let it go.* Whatever it was, whoever it was, it is over. Remember Paul's words to the Romans: "This righteousness from God comes through faith in Jesus Christ to all who believe. There is no difference, for all have sinned and fallen short of the glory of God and are justified freely by God's grace through the redemption that came by Christ Jesus" (Rom. 3:22–24).

Let it go. It is not worth jeopardizing your physical and spiritual health.

Let it go. Decide to go on the journey, to do whatever you need to do, to be free. "It is for freedom that Christ has set us free. Stand firm, then, and *do not let yourselves be burdened again by a yoke of slavery*" (Gal. 5:1, NIV; italics added). Loose it. It is not worth it.

The moment I began the process of letting go of my unforgiving spirit, I began to change. I am not there yet, but I am closer. I am on the journey. Come with me.

Devotion Direction

Review the scriptures noted in this chapter: Galatians 5:1; Ephesians 5:1–2; Matthew 18:21–35; and Romans 10:9.

1. Ask yourself:
   a) Am I harboring an unforgiving spirit? Why? (Write down what you discover; the writing serves as catharsis and as a prayer of beginning.)
   b) How long have I been carrying this?
   c) How has it affected my spirit and my interactions with others?
   d) Why can't I let it go?
2. Ask God to show you *specifically* what to do in order to release this unforgiving spirit from your being. (Again, write it down, and practice God's directives every day.)

four

Let Go of the Fear!

Amanda could not believe it.

She had been in good health all her life, and she did not feel bad now. But to her horror, she discovered a lump under her arm while taking a shower.

Not wanting to believe that she felt it, she tried to make herself believe that it was just extra hardness or something due to her having just ended her period or maybe having exercised too much. That was six months ago. And since that day, that week, she had not touched the spot or even looked at it, as if ignoring it would make it go away.

But here she was, exactly as she had done six months ago, standing in front of her mirror, feeling the blasted thing again. It looked different—maybe bigger. It felt different, too.

She urged herself to stay calm. "It doesn't have to be anything major," she said to herself. "It's probably just a cyst or something." But even though she said the words out loud, she could not make herself believe her alternative. Her mother had died from ovarian cancer; her maternal aunt had died of breast cancer. She knew the stats—she knew she was considered high risk. And in her knowledge, she cried.

Time passed, and still, Amanda had done nothing and said nothing to anyone. She was filled with fear, and it was now controlling her. Every day, she told herself she should call the doctor, but every day she found another reason not to do it. She had been trying to pretend it was nothing. As a way of "fighting" what might be wrong,

Amanda entered into "healthy" eating, and she exercised more. If it was something bad, maybe she could make it go away.

But of course, that approach did not solve her problem, and finally after six more months, she made the painful, scary phone call. After the call, her fear grabbed her more tightly and made her think of all the worst things, such as how her mother had looked as she died. She had noticed her lump and gotten it examined immediately, but in spite of the doctors' assurances that they had "found it early" and had "gotten it all out," her mother had died a brutal, painful death. The once vibrant, energetic woman had wasted down to 95 sick pounds from 140 healthy ones. As the disease progressed, it took over her body. It was in her lymph nodes, in her brain, in her lungs. She had taken the chemotherapy, and it had seemingly made her more sick. Toward the end, her mother could hardly breathe.

Amanda remembered it all in great detail, though it had been years since her mother had died, and as she remembered, she broke down. "I can't go through that!" she wept softly and bitterly. "I can't do it."

But in the midst of her fear, she went to the doctor. It was like a bad dream; Amanda wished that it was. The doctor examined the lump and ordered a biopsy. "How long ago did you notice it?" the doctor asked gently. "Oh, only a couple of days ago," Amanda heard herself saying. "Well, we've scheduled your biopsy for next Tuesday. I'll see you then." The doctor left, and Amanda sat in the examination room feeling alone and scared.

Amanda's worst fears were confirmed by the biopsy. It was cancer, and it had spread. "I'm concerned," said her doctor. "This kind of cancer isn't usually aggressive like this, and yet you said you found it only a few days ago. I don't know exactly how to treat it, but let's believe that we'll catch it before it affects too much more of your body." Amanda's face was white with fear, and the doctor noticed it. "Amanda, don't be afraid. Fear will only make it all worse."

That is the bottom line. Fear only makes things worse.

Fear made Amanda ignore her lump for months, and fear made her lie about how long she had had a problem. Fear made her remember the worst things about her mother's illness and forget that, if caught early enough, many cancers can be managed effectively. Fear may very well have made Amanda lose her life sooner than she might have.

Fear only makes things worse.

What fear have you been carrying? Fear to love someone because you were hurt before? I know, you really loved him, and he really hurt you, but does that mean that everyone will do to you what he did? What if the person you fear now is the person God has sent to you to make you understand that God makes all things new? What if he or she is the blessing you have been waiting for, but you cannot see it and it is about to pass out of your life?

Fear only makes things worse because it makes us operate on myth and not reality. It is said that people who are thrown from horses are encouraged to get back in the saddle as soon as possible before fear makes it impossible for them to do so. Fear has the ability of taking the little things and making them big, or taking the big things and making them impossible. It does so by controlling our minds, not letting us act or react with a childlike innocence or resiliency that gives us the guts to try and try and try again. No, fear locks us in a room, making us see things or hear things or feel things that are not there. It makes us remember past emotions, past experiences, and magnify them a thousand times. In the process, fear keeps us where we are instead of where we should be.

I can remember when I was a child, I had a big bed—one that stood high off the floor. I had watched *Peter Pan,* and although fascinated by the movie, I was terrified by my memory of Captain Hook and that awful crocodile. For some reason, every night, I made myself believe that Captain Hook and the crocodile were coming to get me.

Every night, I had to go to the bathroom, and that was a problem because I was convinced that Captain Hook had put the crocodile under my bed. I can remember getting the urge to "go" every night, closing my eyes, and praying for God to take away the sensation. God did not, and I was faced with the dilemma of how to get from my bed to my door without becoming crocodile food.

Every night, I would look for the crocodile. The only way to see it was to hang over the side of my bed and look under there because I certainly was not going to get out of bed before I caught sight of it. So, I would hang there and look. Even though I could not see it, I was not comforted because my fear told me the thing really was there; I just could not see it. I would look for a long time. The physiological urge to go to the bathroom did not let up, and finally, I had to strategize.

I thought I could not see the crocodile because he was asleep in a corner under the bed. If I was very careful and very quick, I could make it to the door without being apprehended! I took two or three deep breaths and then darted over to the door. My heart rate went up, my breathing was fast, and I had several other problems by that time. But I safely reached the bathroom and reluctantly made my way back to my room. What then? You guessed it. I stood outside my door for the longest time, trying to hear the crocodile. I pushed the door open very slowly and quietly, looking, straining to see it. Finally, though I never saw it, I made a dash for my bed, jumped up on it, and covered my eyes.

Fear only makes things worse.

Of course, there was no crocodile, just as there are no bogeymen in our lives. Yet we reside in fear and surround ourselves with fear. In response, we "sweat" through life and make erroneous decisions, see wrong things, and hear wrong information because we have allowed fear to dictate to us.

We are afraid of all kinds of things. Afraid of our parents. Afraid of confrontation. Afraid of people who do not look like us. Afraid of trying new things, taking new challenges. We are afraid of losing and afraid of winning. Too many of us opt to try neither. We are afraid of trusting, so we do not trust. We are afraid of succeeding, so we sabotage our success. Fear absolutely paralyzes us and keeps us from communion and relationship with God.

Why? Because God is love, and fear is the antithesis of love. Love cannot "digest" fear, and fear cannot receive love. In our fear, we are cut off from the Source of our power, peace, and strength. Fear and love cannot live in the same space, but we do not understand that, and in that misunderstanding, we live "lives of quiet desperation," as Henry David Thoreau once said.

Fear causes God's people to act out of character. People who are jealous, for example, are people driven by fear, and this fear/jealousy makes them see what is not there or hear what is not there. In the process, they act dreadfully and say awful things to the very ones they love most. Many times I have heard a spouse say, "I might as well go ahead and be unfaithful because no matter how hard I try to show him I love him, it doesn't make any difference." The fear/jealousy runs through the relationship like a cancer, and what happens? Usually, the jealous ones lose the persons they are trying to hold on to and may even commit a crime for which they are punished. They lose their self-respect and the respect of their loved ones and children, if there are any. I shake my head when it happens to anyone, but it is especially hard to take when there really was great love between the two people or when the illness of fear strikes very young, teen lovers. Instead of experiencing the ecstasy of love, many end up alone. Fear will absolutely destroy anything of value.

The Bible offers many words of encouragement against fear; we are often urged to "fear not." Perhaps my favorite admonition comes in Isaiah 43, where God said through the prophet, "But now thus says God, the one who created you, O Jacob, the one who formed you, O Israel: *Do not fear,* for I have redeemed you; I have called you by name, *you are mine*" (Isa. 43:1; italics added). God was speaking to the Israelites after God had pretty much wiped out the unfaithful; where there had been fruitfulness and fullness, there were barrenness and blight. It was awful, and the people were understandably worried and afraid.

In the midst of the dryness, in the midst of a situation that could call up the fear of mere mortals, God spoke loudly and clearly: "Fear not." God—you know, the One who created us all—said that. The Creator said, "Don't be afraid." That is like our parents telling us as we try to do something for the first time, "Don't be afraid. I've got you!" Something about that parental reassurance gets us through the times of our lives when, without their assurance, we might never move forward. God said, "Fear not, for I have redeemed you; I have summoned you by name; *you are mine.*" You should not be afraid because Someone greater than you is in control. That Someone loves you, has redeemed you, and knows you by name—in fact, knew you by name before you were born. That Someone has too much invested in you to allow you to suffer. "Fear not."

Then God, through the prophet, continued to explain to us in some of the most comforting words in the Bible that God understands that there are reasons why we might experience fear from time to time. The storms of life. The challenges. The unknowns. The strange lands and eerie-looking paths. *God knows.* So God said,

> *When you pass through the waters,*
>   I will be with you;
> *and through the rivers,*
>   *they shall not overwhelm you;*
> *when you walk through fire*
>   *you shall not be burned,*
>   *and the flame shall not consume you.*

For I am the Sovereign, your God. (Isa. 43:2–3; emphasis added)

The blessed assurance is that (1) God is with us, and (2) God knows what we are going through. What is required on our parts is trusting God so that we can experience the divine presence as we pass through the waters.

Some might protest, "But God isn't here." Yes, God is. The tendency of us Christians to make God transcendent, a nonparticipating member in our everyday lives, is one of the reasons that we suffer. God is "Emmanuel," God with us. Always, God is with us. We feel the iciness of fear when we shut God out and allow ourselves to see and hear with our human eyes and ears as opposed to with our divine beings.

I once asked God something about a relationship during my college days. I wanted the relationship to end because it was not good for me, but I was afraid to let it go. I was afraid of being alone in this couples-oriented society, but after a while, I knew I did not want to be in the relationship. I prayed, "God, help me get out of this, but I don't want to hurt or be depressed when I break it off."

God heard me. I was afraid, and I was paralyzed in that fear, but thank goodness, I had the presence of mind and spirit to call on One greater than myself. I was walking through the fire, and I did not want to be burned. God worked it out. It happened that I was at this person's house, and in the middle of the night, God woke me and said, "Go home." I listened and obeyed. I had an old rusty car that operated on faith, and I was not sure that in the subzero weather, it would start. But amazingly, it did. It got me home, but before I could turn it off, it stopped—*right in front of my house!* I went inside and went to sleep. I did not feel bad, but I knew that my relationship was over. The car never started again, I never saw the guy again, and I did not drop one single tear. The experience was amazing.

When we give God our fear, God does things with it that we could never hope to do. God is with us all the time. In Matthew 8:23–27 (NIV), Jesus shows us how true this is. Jesus got into a boat after teaching some followers of the cost of being a disciple. Then "without warning," a storm came up on the lake. The storm was so furious that the waves "swept over the boat." Do you know what Jesus did? He was asleep when the storm rose up, and he remained asleep. *But he was still with them.*

The disciples, not knowing the value of the presence of Jesus, went to him in fear and woke him up. "Lord, save us! We're going to drown!" With such a cry of anxiety, one might have expected Jesus to react with empathy and gentleness. Instead, he was irritated. He said, "You of little faith, why are you so afraid?" Then he got up and rebuked the winds and the waves, and *it was completely calm.*

Having Jesus as Sovereign and Savior means that you have a way out of fear. You do not have to stay where you are, paralyzed by the demon of fear. You do not have to keep thinking that the storms in your life have more power over you than they actually do. If you can let fear go for a moment, replace it with faith, and in that faith, call on God, then God will rebuke the storm and make it possible for you to survive in good stead and with a healthy spirit.

To be released from this fear, you have to begin practicing your faith in ways you never have before. You have to take the proverbial "one step" so that God can take two. And in that tentative first step, you have to say something like "I can do this" or "I can do all things through Christ who strengthens me." You have to *say* that you do not have to be afraid because your ultimate Parent knows you by name, knows who you are and what you need. Your ultimate Parent is in the storm with you and will not let it overtake you. You just have to believe it, and a good way to believe is to say it over and over.

Does all this seem silly? Yes? Well, haven't you had to talk yourself through many challenges of life? Did you have to talk yourself into not being afraid of getting married? Especially the second time, when you remembered so clearly the failure and the pain of the first? Did you have to talk yourself into not being afraid that going to the doctor would mean that you were about to hear your death sentence? Did you have to talk yourself into not being afraid to apply to college or maybe to medical school, something you had wanted to do for a long time? If you have done it, you know it works, and all I ask is that on this journey, you use God and God's words to walk you through the valley of fear to victory.

At the end of these forty days, I want other travelers on this journey to have testimonies that they started out too afraid to even think, but they used God—Emmanuel—called on God's name, trusted God, replaced fear with faith, and were rewarded. It is the only way to please God. Remember, in the midst of that storm, Jesus was not touched by his disciples' confidence in him to save them; he was irritated that they would think he would let the storm consume them in the first place.

Even as I write this, I feel liberated. "Perfect love drives out fear" (1 John 4:18, NIV). On this journey, you and I have to embrace perfect love and head into the storm. It will be okay.

By the way, "Amanda" did not make it. Her fear led to her early death.

Devotion Direction

1. Identify the thing or things you are afraid of. Ask yourself:
   a) Where did it come from?
   b) How long have I feared it?
   c) How is it affecting my life?

2. Begin to write a personal narrative of your spiritual journey and how it has been affected by this fear.

3. Identify the things in your life that have been adversely affected by your fear. Have you lost a relationship because of it? A job? An opportunity?

4. Read Matthew 8:23–27. How do you think Jesus is reacting to your fear? Have you ever expressed it to him?

5. Write a prayer about your fear that you can say nightly. Record in your journal how saying this prayer, and believing in God's power through this prayer, is affecting your fear and your life.

five

When There Is Not Enough Faith

It is so hard to keep on believing when all the odds, everything on earth, says it's foolish to do so.

Ko-Ko Bear was a beautiful Siberian husky. She had been the family dog forever. Frisky and playful, she was a delight to watch. Instead of barking, she had this wonderful way of "talking"—meaning she made the most incredible sounds and moved her head and somehow got people to understand her. She was red and white, with blue eyes, and gentle, so gentle. Even when the younger children in the family would ride her and tie ribbons around her at Christmas, and the littlest one would try to put her in her doll's baby buggy, Ko-Ko Bear patiently endured.

She had never been sick, except when Sophie, the other family dog, had tragically died of a liver disease. Ko-Ko was grief-stricken. Her family got home one day and found her lying on the back porch, panting and near death. Rushing her to the vet, they learned what had happened: in her distress, she had been eating everything in sight—wood, nails, metal. The veterinarian didn't have time to do her surgery that evening, but he gave her a sedative so she wouldn't wake up or try to go to the bathroom for the night, and advised the family to take her home and bring her back in the morning. The next day she had the surgery, and soon she was back to normal.

That had been Ko-Ko Bear's one brush with death. Other than that, she seemed strong as an ox.

Well, time passed, and Ko-Ko grew old. The family tried not to be gone for long stretches, because they didn't want to leave her in the house alone for too long. One summer day, though, they had been out a little longer than usual and had some trepidation as they hurried home.

When they got home, they called her, but she didn't come. That wasn't too surprising, because she was so old she was going deaf and they frequently had to call her several times before she came. After the fourth call, they began to worry a little. "Go look for her," Katrina, the mother, told her young son.

Katrina thought she might have to clean up a little, but nothing in her consciousness prepared her for what came next. "Mommie!" screamed her young son. Katrina hurried up to her room, where Ko-Ko always slept by the side of the bed, and gasped at what she saw.

There was blood everywhere. It was unmistakably blood; the carpet was white and left no room for doubt. Blood. Everywhere. And there was Ko-Ko, lying listless on the floor, panting.

"Oh, pretty Ko-Ko, what's wrong?" Katrina asked, her shaking voice betraying the fear she felt. She was struggling not to cry. She didn't want her children to see that she was afraid, but the dog looked as though she would die at any moment. "What's wrong, Ko-Ko?"

The dog could barely lift her head. Her eyes were sad and tired. Katrina urged her to stand up, fearing she wouldn't be able to. With lots of effort, Ko-Ko finally stood, and the frightened family led her to the backyard.

Trying to find out how sick the dog was, Katrina shook her car keys, just to see if she could get a response. Ko-Ko loved to ride. "Want to go bye-bye?" Katrina asked. But there was nothing. "Go get her some water," Katrina said to her twelve-year-old daughter, but Ko-Ko took nothing. The smell of a hamburger didn't sway her. The suggestion of a walk didn't move her. It looked as though Ko-Ko was going to die.

The children started to cry, but Katrina, in desperation, said, "No, no! She'll be OK. We have to believe she'll be OK." Inside, she was screaming at herself, "What do you mean, she'll be OK? She's bleeding to death, for goodness' sake!" But her faith told her to believe in the impossible, that "without faith it was impossible to please God." So she gathered her two children, and on a summer's night in their backyard, they prayed for Ko-Ko's life.

"Now, you've got to believe that God heard and that God will heal her," said Katrina. "All we can do now is wait." So the three-some went into the house, and Katrina drove to the grocery store to buy some white vinegar. There was still the blood to remove from the white bedroom carpet.

On the way to the store, she cried. She didn't know how she'd cope with the grief of her children at losing their beloved family pet, much less her own feelings of loss. The tears flowed; Katrina could not stop them. "Please, God, save Ko-Ko," she whispered.

She arrived home and went to work immediately on cleaning the carpet. After a few moments, she heard a small voice. "Mom, is Ko-Ko going to die?"

Katrina answered so quickly that she startled herself. "No, she'll be OK. We'll take her to the vet in the morning. We just have to believe that God will do what God can do!"

After she cleaned the carpet, Katrina went out to the backyard. Ko-Ko was lying as far away from the house as possible—as if she was trying to be alone as she died. Katrina called her name softly, but there was no response. She rubbed her fluffy fur and kissed her nose. "Be OK, Ko-Ko," she whispered.

Katrina was about to get up when she heard Something inside her tell her to pray for the dog one more time. "Lay your hands on her and pray" is what she heard. She paused. She had never done anything like this before—and besides, wasn't this sort of thing meant for people, not dogs? And anyway, who was she? But the command seemed so compelling that she obeyed it. "God, I don't know if this is sacrilegious or not, but please, hear me. Please heal my dog." Katrina prayed as she never had before. After a few moments, she stopped and looked at Ko-Ko. There was no movement. Nothing. No change. Katrina got up, and she heard the Something say, "Now, leave it alone. Believe that it will be done." Everything in her wanted to argue. Everything in her wanted to protest and say, "Look at her! She's barely breathing, for heaven's sake!" But that Something said, "Go inside and don't look back. It's in my hands now."

So she went inside, and she told her children that faith meant letting go and believing. "We can't worry now," she said to them. "Faith and fear cannot exist in the same space." So they went to bed.

Several times during the night, Katrina got up and went to her son's bedroom window, looking for Ko-Ko. She couldn't see her, and wanted to go outside, but that Something said, "No." So after the third time, she made herself stay in bed, concentrating on believing.

The next morning, Katrina got up early and went outside, afraid of what she'd find. If Ko-Ko was dead, she didn't want the children to see her. "God, please let me be able to handle this," she prayed silently. But to her surprise, when she approached the dog, Ko-Ko was lying down, panting, but her head was up and her paws were stretched out in front of her. She wagged her tail a little as she saw Katrina approach. Katrina couldn't believe her eyes. She brought the dog some water, and Ko-Ko drank slowly. Katrina began to cry. While this wasn't a healing, it was surely better than the night before.

"Maybe she's going to die but just not right away," said Katrina to herself. "The kids will have time to see her kind of normal first." And sure enough, when they woke up and came outside, they rejoiced at what they saw.

The morning passed, and Katrina called the vet to make an appointment for the afternoon. But when it was time to go, Ko-Ko was acting normal—a little weak, but normal. She wanted to eat. She wanted to go for a ride. She wanted to go for a walk. She did her famous "talking"!

Skeptical, Katrina took her to the appointment. After the exam, the veterinarian said, "Well, I don't know what happened to her last night . . . but right now, she's perfectly healthy." And right there, in front of everyone, Katrina broke down, realizing for the first time the power of faith.

Okay, you may not have a sick dog, but is there something that you are struggling with that requires you to have a little more faith? Is there something about which you have so much doubt that your thoughts are getting in the way of God's work?

Because that is what faithlessness is: a hindrance to God's work. Our ways and God's ways are not the same; we all know that. But we want God's way and ours to be the same, and when that is not the case—or when it seems that God is taking too long to come over to *our* way of thinking—we sink into doubt. It is called faithlessness.

In case you did not know it, that is part of what is meant by blaspheming the Holy Spirit. Blaspheming the Holy Spirit is the one sin that cannot be forgiven, says the Bible, and what this means is that *if we doubt that the Holy Spirit has the power to do whatever Jesus asks of it, we in effect doubt the power of Christ.* In this doubt, we also leave ourselves open to influence by the Paraclete. To doubt the Holy Spirit (blaspheme) is to replace divine ability with human thought, which is so full of limits. The human mind cannot begin to comprehend what the Holy Spirit is able to do, but to doubt that it can do whatever it pleases, being part of God, is to commit the sin of pride and to put oneself on the same plane as God. It seems that the more we believe in the impossible, the more the Holy Spirit surprises our human inclinations and consciousness!

Faith requires us to believe that the Spirit of God, which sustains us and feeds us, is omnipotent. Faith requires us to believe that for God, or with God, *nothing* is impossible. We are required to believe that God really can make a way out of no way, and the evidence of our belief in that truth should come out in the way that we present our lives to God.

One of the reasons that faithlessness takes over too many of us is that we misunderstand what the relationship between God and us must be. God is not a magician; God is a Spirit with whom we are supposed to be in communication. In that communication, we talk, we listen, and we learn God's ways. In that learning, we gain confidence or faith, and it grows only as the relationship between God and us grows. We develop a trust in God that carries us through the bad times. It is no different really from what we do as we develop relationships with people. The more we talk and communicate, the more the trust grows and the better the relationship. When things happen that are difficult to understand, we are able to better cope and not fly off the handle and believe the worst because the relationship is intact.

Unfortunately, we do not do that with God. Instead, we sort of use the Divine when it is convenient. Consequently, we do not know God, and God really has not been allowed to know us. We do not know how God works or what God expects from us. We consider God as a big Something in the great Somewhere who is supposedly able to do great things.

When something happens that requires faith, we are at a loss. And I do not suppose that God feels compelled to come running to our aid!

Being faithful does not mean that you believe that everything will always go the way you want it. It is the assurance, though, that God will hear you and give you what you need in order to get through a situation. It is the assurance that whatever happens is in God's hands and that God is walking with you.

I remember when I was pregnant with my son. It had been a normal pregnancy, but one day, I got a call from my obstetrician. It was necessary for me to have a special diagnostic ultrasound.

"Why?" I asked as I visited with my doctor in his office.

He paused, clearly uncomfortable. "Because it seems that in your last ultrasound, we picked up something." He stopped.

"Picked up what?" I asked, now alarmed.

He paused again. "Susan, your child may be hydrocephalic."

I was stunned. I could not say anything for a moment. Then I asked, "Are you sure?"

"No," he said, "but I have to tell you, it doesn't look good."

I was not prepared for the situation. I drove back to work in a daze, went into my office, and closed the door. I pulled the blinds to shut out the light and just sat there. The tears started. They came and came and came. I cried as hard as I ever have.

"Oh, God, oh, God," I kept saying. But in the midst of that weak little prayer, I heard God talk back to me. Only when you are in relationship with God can you hear God. And I heard God say, "Be quiet. It's okay."

The voice was so clear that it stunned me. I stopped crying and listened again. God repeated the message, and a calm came over me. From that moment, I knew that whatever the ultrasound showed, God had the situation under control.

As I moved toward the day of the diagnostic ultrasound, I was amazed at how calm I continued to be. I was not worried because of what God had told me.

When I went into the special doctor's office, with the special tools and gadgets and equipment, I was okay. As I climbed up on the table for the exam, the doctor entered the room and said to me, "Well, hello, Mrs. Smith. Do you know why you're here?"

Anxious for the exam to be over (you have to drink a lot of water prior to the test and I was very uncomfortable), I answered, "Oh, yes, I know. My doctor thinks that my child might be hydrocephalic, but I already know better. God has already told me that he is okay."

The doctor looked at me with pity in his eyes. I knew that he was thinking that I was yet another potential parent in denial. He had seen many and knew better than to argue. I wanted to say again, "It *is* okay. God told me!" I was so sure. But the man began the procedure and everything got quiet, so I did, too.

He moved the instrument back and forth, up and down. The room was dark. I could see the outline of my child on the screen. I could not tell what I was seeing, only that he was moving a lot. The doctor looked and looked, wrote something down, and looked some more. I just wanted it to be over.

After a while, he said, "Okay," and walked out of the room. I wasn't to move, said the nurse. He might have to look some more. So, I lay there uncomfortable, but full of faith.

When he came back in, he had a strange look on his face. "Mrs. Smith, I don't know how you knew it, but this baby is perfectly normal!"

"YEEESSS!" I knew it! I told him so, too. "I knew it, Doctor. I told you that God said it would be okay."

The doctor said, "But he has such a big head!"

I put my hands on my head and said, "Look! That's normal for us. We come from a big-headed family. And you haven't even seen his daddy's head."

Having faith produces miracles. The miracle in that experience was my peace *before* I knew the outcome of that diagnostic ultrasound. Whatever happened would have been okay because God had given me divine assurance that whatever it was would be okay. Through my relationship with God, I received the miracle of the peace that passes all understanding.

"But," you say, "God came through for you. God did not come through for me!" You prayed that your mother would not die from cancer, but she did. You prayed that your child would recover from a rare disease, but he did not. Or God "abandoned" you when God allowed your child to be killed by a classmate. You prayed for a different outcome, and yet what? You do not have faith because you have been praying for a job for a long time and you still do not have it. Or you have been praying for enough money to make ends meet, but it has not happened. Your utilities have been turned off, you do not have any food, and God has done nothing.

I beg to differ. God has not always answered my prayers the way I wanted them answered. I have been disappointed by the divine answers; nevertheless, I can say that I know God has always been with me. God's relationship with me has been my saving grace. God is a divine Parent, and just as we, as human parents, do not give our children everything they ask for, we give them everything they *need*. God is the same way, and the more we develop our relationship and the better it becomes, the better becomes our track record in receiving what we want. It becomes better not because God is necessarily doing more but because we can recognize what God is doing or can do. We believe that God can and will handle our situation, and we in essence let go of ourselves and let God take control.

Having faith makes things happen; not having it prevents things from happening. I am amazed every time I consider the story of Mary McLeod Bethune, a black woman in a white, male-dominated world who *believed* that she could build a school. Even as she gazed upon her land, a former garbage heap, and realized she did not have even the beginnings of the money she would need to fulfill her dream, she *believed*. I am equally amazed at the story of Alexander Graham Bell, who *believed* that he could make a "talking machine," or at the story of Arthur Mitchell, who *believed* that he could form a successful African American classical ballet company. People who believe see miracles every day, and God wants us all to have that experience.

God can do anything God wants, and God wants us to believe it. And when we do not believe, our divine Parent becomes angry. When the disciples could not drive out a demon from a little boy, they asked Jesus why. He replied, "*Because you have so little faith. If you have faith as small as a mustard seed, you can say to this mountain, 'Move from here to there,' and it will move. Nothing will be impossible for you*" (Matt. 17:20, NIV; italics added). We have to believe, even when believing is hard; otherwise, it is called faithlessness, and I repeat, it irritates God.

In the first chapter of Luke, the angel of God appeared to Zechariah to tell him of the impending birth of a son to him and his wife, Elizabeth. Zechariah found the tale quite far-fetched. After listening, he said, "How can I be sure of this? I am an old man and my wife is well along in years" (v. 18, NIV).

God has patience, but only a little, when we doubt like that. Speaking on God's behalf, the angel told Zechariah, "I am Gabriel. I stand in the presence of God and I have been sent to speak to you and to tell you the good news. And now you will be silent and not able to speak until the day this happens *because you did not believe my words* which will come true at their proper time" (vv. 19–20, NIV; italics added).

God had a similar reaction to an officer in Elisha's army when God said, "'About this time tomorrow, a seah of flour will sell for a shekel and two seahs of barley for a shekel at the gate of Samaria.' The officer on whose arm the king was leaning said to the man of God, 'Look, even if [God] should open the floodgates of the heavens, could this happen?' 'You will see it with your eyes,' answered Elisha, 'but you shall not eat any of it'" (2 Kings 7:1–2, NIV). God again reacted with irritation when the officer did not believe.

During these forty days, you have to let go of your faithlessness. That means you will have to let go of the emotions that make you remember your disappointment with God and begin to concentrate on the ways God has blessed you. You will have to agree to enter into a relationship with God, which further means that your prayer during these forty days might have to be, "God, show me how to do that!" You will have to lay out before God the reasons you have so little faith. You and God together will have to examine that situation, and you will have to let God guide you to a place of peace from the torment you now feel. In some way, you will have to remember that God is on your side, that God wants you to be blessed and feel blessed. If you agree to enter a relationship with God, you will feel the divine presence and at least move nearer to hearing God's voice. You will have blessed assurance. It is a journey, but if you believe and do not doubt that this journey can help you shake off this pain of faithlessness, you will be blessed.

Devotion Direction

1. Study these examples of faithlessness: Genesis 19:14; 2 Kings 7:2; Isaiah 53:1; Matthew 13:58; and Luke 22:67. How did God react in each episode?

2. Answer this question in your journal: Why am I experiencing faithlessness? How did it come about? When? What have I done to correct it?

3. Examine your relationship with God. Answer the following questions:

   a) When do I pray, or how have I prayed up to this point?

   b) Do I expect or have I expected to hear from God?

   c) In my praying, am I always talking but never listening? Can I build a relationship in that way?

six

Shaking Loose of the Green-Eyed Monster

He did not want to feel what he was feeling. Eliza was "his" woman. She had declared her love for him countless times and in countless ways. She was always there for him, always smiling, always, it seemed, giving from deep within. It seemed that her whole desire was to please him.

She had never shown interest in another man. He knew that because it did not happen when she was with him, and he had inquired enough to know that it had not happened when she was without him, either. As beautiful as she was, she never flirted or led anyone on. Any man would want her; the point is, she did not want *any* man. She wanted him.

And yet he was not comfortable. It was as though he was consumed. When she was not around, he wondered where she was or whether she was really where she said she was going to be, although she had never given him a reason to doubt her actions. If she did not get home when she said she was going to be home, he would call and call and call, partially because he was worried that something might have happened to her, but more because he was concerned that perhaps she was with someone else.

If she smiled at anyone—male or female—he grew jealous. He wanted all of her attention, all of the time. If she talked to anyone and did not seem to notice him for a few minutes, he steamed with anger. If she thought a man on television or a movie was talented or good-looking, and she said so, he was angry.

He tried to shake it, but it was like a demon, hanging on to him and draining him of common sense and logic. He felt sometimes that he wanted to tie her up or put bars at the doors and windows, just so he would be sure that she was really his.

He had been good, he thought, at hiding it. She had no idea his jealousy was so intense. Oh, she was annoyed when he would call and call and call anytime she did not answer the phone right away, but she tried to deal with it. And she was very clear about where she was going and how long she would be gone, though sometimes she thought he went overboard. But for the most part, she did not know about this gnawing feeling within him that seemed to be growing deeper and more pervasive with each day.

Even in church, he was not comfortable. When she had given the minister a hug a couple of weeks ago, he had almost bitten through his lip, he was so jealous. He derided himself for immediately wondering if there was something between them. He derided himself even more for making himself believe that every man wanted his wife. Even if that was the case, he mused, shouldn't that make him proud and not so insecure, since she never acknowledged anyone but him?

He was really getting nervous about himself. He had never felt so out of control. Had he been this way in high school? He thought back, and sure enough, he had been what they called possessive. He had never been able to hold on to a relationship because this jealousy thing would get in the way and make him do and say stupid things. He did not want to be this way, and yet he did not know how to stop it.

Well, he was scared now. He was scared because the longer he was with her, the harder it was for him to let her out of his sight, and he knew that he would lose her if he kept it up. He did not know what to do; he did not know how to correct himself. He was too embarrassed to tell anyone about his "problem," and as a result, he felt trapped between his rational mind and his irrational being. Whatever was he going to do? He was really worried.

· · ·

"Jealousy" is defined as being "fearful or wary of being supplanted; possessively watchful or vigilant," according to the *American Heritage Dictionary*. It is indeed a monster. A little jealousy from time to time may be considered normal, for example, when your mother praises your sister for something she did that you already did but did not even get noticed. Or perhaps a little jealousy is warranted when you, the pregnant wife, see your husband eyeing a nonpregnant damsel—a perfect size ten—as she walks past the two of you.

But when the jealousy becomes a way of life, when it becomes one of those "powers and principalities" vying for control of your spirit and your body, you are in deep trouble.

It comes from fear—the demon within us that gives rise to so many toxic emotions and attitudes. Jealousy is the fear that someone may take your place, that someone may garner more attention, more love, more of what you want, and that you will not be important enough or be enough, period, to beat the threat.

Why are you so jealous? What sorts of things has it led you to do? Don't you want to stop feeling so out of control?

To stop the jealousy, you have to identify where it came from. When did it rear its ugly head, and why?

You may be jealous because you have been burned before, and you cannot shake the memory. This kind of jealousy might be present in relationships. You remember how badly it hurt. You were deeply in love with her, were loyal to her, gave her all she wanted and more, and still, she cheated on you. You can remember when you found out about her betrayal and how it devastated you. At first you denied it; ignoring it made you feel better. But as time went on, the situation grew worse, and she seemed to throw it in your face and almost dared you to do anything. Like a defeated animal, you backed away, shocked, hurt, mortified, and angry. For the next few years, nobody could get next to you. You could go for a while, but then the memory of what she did to you would flood your being, and you would do something to sabotage the relationship. You had been doing it for so long that it became habit; unconsciously, you ended a relationship before it really got started. But you told yourself it did not matter because you would never love again.

Now, though, you are smitten. Despite your best efforts, you have someone you really love, and try as hard as you will, you cannot let go of the jealousy. Your fear has bred its child, jealousy, and it is ruining your life.

Maybe you are jealous because when you were little, you never got attention from your parents, and you have tried to excel since then to be noticed. So, you have always been a superachiever. Your drive for attention has made you extremely competitive and jealous, and your jealousy is so bad that when it seems that someone will step ahead of you, you will do almost anything to sabotage that person. When the sabotage has not worked, you have fumed and decided that you did not like that person, going so far as to make up lies or do things to make him or her uncomfortable. You have watched the person's career carefully, being glad when you have seen trouble or a glitch. In spite of your best efforts, you have actually heard yourself laughing at his or her misfortune or wishing something would happen to slow the person down. Jealousy is guiding your life. You are still a little child trying to get your mother's or father's attention, and in your parents' absence, you fight frantically for your due.

Maybe you are jealous because you never liked yourself or how you looked, and you have decided that everyone looks better than you. Incredible! Instead of taking time to do more with yourself, you have devoted time to rolling your eyes at people you have decided "think" they look better than you. You are unkind to them; in high school you started fights with them. You made up your mind that they deserved to be taught a lesson by you just because you never realized that you are "fearfully and wonderfully made" (Ps. 139:14, NIV).

Come on! Aren't you tired of comparing yourself, putting yourself down, being worried about your mate and his or her whereabouts? Aren't you tired of believing that you are less than you are? Aren't you tired of being led around by "the monster"?

We can see examples in the Bible of jealousy and its effects on people. There is the story of Joseph and his brothers (Gen. 37, NIV). According to the Word, "Israel loved Joseph more because he was born to him in his old age," and he made Joseph a richly ornamented robe (Gen. 37:3). The next verse is critical: "When his brothers saw that their father loved him more than any of them, they hated him and could not speak a kind word to him." Jealousy—it made them *hate* their brother and be unable to speak a kind word to him. Taken further, it made their resentment boil up and make things up about him that were not true; they had to conjure up behavior on his part that justified their actions. They lied to him and about him in order to support their jealous feelings.

It seems that Joseph had the ability to interpret dreams, and his talent made his brothers hate him all the more. The last straw was Joseph's dream in which they were all binding sheaves of grain, but his sheaf stood up while theirs gathered around his and bowed down to it. The jealousy of the brothers erupted into raw, open anger.

"Do you think you'll rule over us?" they asked menacingly, yet really afraid. "Do you actually intend to rule over us?" (vv. 6–8). They hated him even more, and though the Bible does not say it, they probably muttered among themselves that he was an arrogant, spoiled brat who needed to be taught a lesson.

Joseph did not improve the situation. As if blind to their feelings, he told them yet another dream in which the "sun and moon and stars were bowing down" to him (vv. 9–10). His brothers "were jealous of him" (v. 11), and that was putting it mildly.

What had the jealousy spawned? Anger. Fear. (Isn't it interesting that fear breeds jealousy, which in turn breeds more fear?) Resentment. Sibling rivalry. Antagonism within the family. Murderous intent. The young men, Joseph's brothers, were not bad men. They were just not in control. Jealousy had them and was playing havoc with their peace of mind and with their presence of mind. Isn't that what happens with jealous spouses? Is it jealousy that spawns in a man a rage so terrible that he from time to time hits his spouse and hurts her when he in fact loves her?

The brothers were not in control, and in their impulsive state, they plotted to kill Joseph. And so those "nice" boys stripped Joseph of the robe their father had made him and threw Joseph into a well. There was no water in it, but it was deep. They knew their brother would not be able to get out unless he had help from others. They pondered leaving him there to die, but then his brother Judah suggested it would do them no good to let him die; they decided instead to sell him as a slave to the Ishmaelites. In a split second, the "nice" boys, governed by "the monster," had turned into monsters themselves.

Have you been there? Are you there now? You cannot stay there and be whole. You cannot stay there and call yourself Christian. Those feelings of jealousy are antithetical to what Christian love is all about. What are you going to do?

To reach victory, you have to reveal, first to yourself and then to God, why you are carrying such toxic emotions. It is very hard sometimes to look at ourselves and see what God sees, see the reasons why the gifts of grace and mercy are so incredible. A stain on your spirit that was put there a long time ago is blocking you from peace of mind. What is it, and how did it get there?

To reveal yourself, you have to trust God. God already knows what you are feeling and why, but God wants you to be brave enough and to trust the divine powers of love and forgiveness to pull you through your pain toward release. God stands ready to catch your tears, your emotions, your questions, as you make your way back and then forward again. That feeling of jealousy did not get there overnight, nor did it get there in a vacuum.

The questions you may have to ask yourself may hurt. For example, if you are jealous because of a cheating spouse, you have to ask yourself, What did I do to contribute to the situation? Nothing happens in a vacuum, and if you are careful to examine yourself, you can usually see your role. It is more comfortable to simply blame the other person, but if you are going to heal, the blame has to stop today. In the story of Joseph and his brothers, how convenient it would have been for Joseph to point a wounded finger toward them and say, "They did me wrong!" But I do not think he did that. I think that to be able to show them forgiveness, he had to first experience the forgiveness that God had given him for being so insensitive to them and their needs. In order to heal, you have to reveal your part in the situation.

Next, in order to heal, you have to accept God's instructions about how you are to move from this point. For example, if your self-examination indicates that your spouse cheated because you were too possessive, then you will have to trust God when God says, "Lean on *my* arms! Don't let her (or him) define your life; let me!" Being possessive is a sin in that it separates us from God, and anything that separates us from God is a sin. Being possessive means that you wanted that man or that woman more than you wanted God, and God will not have that. Maybe you did not have a God-consciousness when you were in relationship with him or her. God will say to you to let go of anything or anyone that you place above God. God will say to you to trust God more than any human being, and if you want to heal, you will have to do that.

Third, you will have to agree to love yourself just as you are, and therefore not compare yourself to others so that you might become jealous of others. God loves you just as you are; you are enough, you are adequate, just as you are. If God loves you, you should love yourself and lose the fear that leads to jealousy. In this journey, you will have to agree to leave your past behind you, the past that has prevented you from appreciating your innate value and therefore kept you in a competitive mode and in a jealous mood.

Whoever did not pay attention to you when you were young— it does not matter. God pays attention to you all the time. Whoever cheated on you—it does not matter. If you trust God, God will send you someone who will not cheat on you, but more important, God will never cheat on you. And God's love for you is so great that God will do all that God can do to make sure you get the best. When you love God, God will show you how much God loves you, and somehow, that fact is able to keep you grounded, secure, and unafraid.

I am convinced that developing a strong relationship with God is the only way to erase jealousy. We read in Isaiah 26:3, "Those of steadfast mind you keep in peace—in peace because they trust in you." The transformation of one who is jealous to one who is comfortable and secure is no less radical a transformation than that of a drug addict to one who is clean. This journey will not be easy. You will find yourself making forward progress and then slip back, and you will have to pray and seek God as you never have before. Just because you say you want to be healed does not mean the healing will come overnight. No, this will be a process—and a tedious one at that. Your biggest foe will be yourself, but if you want to be healed, you will be. If you are steadfast, you will one day have the testimony that you have been changed; you will find that the jealousy is finally gone and that you can experience the blessings that God has placed in your life without all the pain and insecurity.

A final note: you work toward this healing because jealousy is detrimental to the peace of your spirit, and it is displeasing to God. I repeat, you cannot be jealous and fail to work on it and still call yourself a Christian. Being a Christian means that you are willing to "repent," which means to change, and to "repent" of anything that is not pleasing to God. When Miriam and Aaron were jealous of Moses (Num. 12) and mumbled against him, God was angry and "left them"; Miriam suddenly developed leprosy, and God would not heal her for seven days. God watches us and wants us to realize the things we carry that keep us away from God. So, you see, your acknowledgment of your jealousy is not an option; it is a spiritual obligation that you must undertake in order to experience victory.

God will keep you in perfect peace. Now, begin the journey. *What made you so jealous in the first place?*

Devotion Direction

Read Genesis 37.

1. Your jealousy is an obstacle meant to be defeated. Do you want to defeat it?

2. How did jealousy change the personalities of Joseph's brothers? How has your jealousy changed your personality?

3. List three things that your jealousy has made you say or do for which you are sorry.

4. What is your part in feeling what you feel? How have you contributed to the situations that provoke your jealousy?

5. Have you shared your feelings with God? Can you begin to do so?

6. What are you most afraid of? What do you think you must do to shake the fear?

seven

Be Anxious for Nothing

Mary did not know what she was going to do. She was recently divorced, the mother of three children. Her divorce had been unexpected on her part. She and her husband had experienced difficulties, to be sure, but never once had she considered that things were seriously wrong. Yes, she noticed that he did not talk much to her—or that they did not talk much together anymore—but she attributed that to their busyness. And she also realized that they almost never went out anywhere together, but again, she found an excuse. They were too tired most of the time, dealing with the children, to go out. Things were okay, she rationalized. He came home every night, and they were a family.

Mary's world was shattered when one day he came home while she was doing the laundry and announced, as he gave her the keys to the second car, that he was leaving her. She remembered her reaction, even now. She was dumfounded! Surely, she heard wrong. She searched his face and looked for a sign that it was a joke—a sick one, but a joke nonetheless. But there was no merriment in his eyes. He was dead serious.

As she stood there groping for something to say, she heard him say that he had not felt that she loved him for a long time, that he had not felt supported. She heard him say that it was too unbearable for him, and that he was leaving. And yes, there was somebody else.

She did not know what to do or what to say. Should she be angry or sad or what? She could not conjure up her "correct" emotional response. And so she watched him as he took a lone suitcase with him and told her he would come back to get his things when she and the children were not there.

That day, maybe the next few days, had been like a dream for Mary. But slowly, she began to emerge from the cloud. As she realized what had happened—that her husband had actually left her for another woman—she went through a whole range of emotions, including anger, bitterness, self-blame, and shock. She could not believe that her life, as she had known it, was ending.

She was still in a transition mode until one day, Donald, her oldest child, asked her, "Mom, what's going to happen to us? Are we going to have to move?" For some reason, Mary had not dealt with the reality in its fullest sense until she heard his question. "My God," she whispered, "what *is* going to happen to us?"

Mary had never worked. She had dropped out of college her second year when the young, dashing intern had asked her to marry him. Never, since then, had she wanted for anything. They had a wonderful lifestyle. Mary never worked and never worried.

But this new thing was making everything different. Her husband did not want to pay the amount of alimony it would take for her to stay in their house. Figuring up her bills, Mary realized that for the first time in her life, she would have to work outside the home. Doing what? She panicked. "What can I do?" she wailed.

As she began to handle all the things that came with a broken marriage—finding an attorney, getting things in her own name, and trying to remain a sane adult in the process—Mary realized that the kind of job she would need to keep the house, pay for child care, and have a little extra money for survival, well, that kind of job did not exist for her. Clerical skills. Employers needed employees with those skills. Clerical skills and computer literacy. She was going to have to go to school to learn them. Where was the money going to come from?

She was scared. She did not know how to handle this house situation. She certainly did not want to live in an apartment, not after living in such a fine house, but she was not going to be able to buy a house. Not now. She had no money and no credit. God help her if she needed anything major. The same problem—no money and no credit—still applied.

And yet the Word says, "Do not be anxious about anything, but in everything, by prayer and petition, with thanksgiving, present your requests to God. And the peace of God, which transcends all understanding, will guard your hearts and your minds in Christ Jesus" (Phil. 4:6–7, NIV).

Was the writer of that great epistle kidding when he wrote the magnificent words? How can one *not* worry when a situation like Mary's is looming and there appears to be no human solution?

As you ponder that question, I want you to also ponder the reality that when the avalanches of life happen, no human solutions are going to work unless and until your spiritual being takes over. Unless and until you learn to "let go and let God" lead you in this valley in which you now sit, you will not emerge.

Those who live the fullest lives are those who realize that being with God is not something we merely say; it is something we learn to do, and the process should deepen every day. The quest for us as Christians is to be in constant communication with God, receiving our direction from God. That requires a letting go of our human pride, our human arrogance, our fear and insecurity, and trusting this Spirit we cannot see, touch, or feel. Some Christians say they love God, but the love cannot be real unless and until complete surrender to God takes place. And that takes desire, patience, and trust.

The *desire* that must happen is that we must want the Sovereign Jesus more than we want anything else in life—more than a husband or a wife, more than a relationship, more than our children, or more than a high-paying job. We have to want to be a part of the realm of God more than we want anything else and be willing to do whatever it takes to have that experience.

I remember when I was quite a bit younger, and I wanted a relationship. Rev. Barbara Allen, the assistant minister at Trinity United Church of Christ in Chicago, took me aside and said, "Susan, you want the wrong things. The Bible says to 'seek ye first the realm of God and all these other things will be added unto you!'" I listened to her and protested, "But I don't *want* the realm of God! I want this relationship!" Well, I have grown since then, and I have learned that inclusion in God's realm is the most blessed experience one can have. In that realm are gifts not experienced by those outside the gates. The realm is open to us all who profess the Sovereign Jesus, but we have to *desire* it with everything we have.

Complete surrender to Jesus also requires *patience*. It might seem unfair that we have to wait a moment before we realize the power that comes from surrendering to Jesus, but he really waits—and therefore we wait—to see if we are serious. In a moment of emotional turmoil, we can say, "O my God, please help me!" But when the crisis is over, what? Do we go back into our "I'll get with God later" attitudes? Jesus considers communion with him too precious for the fickle. He wants us to want to be with him completely in good times and in bad; during the crises and after we reach the mountaintop. Anything less is not acceptable. Often we have to wait to feel the effect of having confessed him. Many people are reluctant to wait. Because the change they seek does not come immediately, they back away. How many times have people joined a church with a burden on their hearts, thinking that since they have joined, everything will be all right tomorrow—only to find that is not the case? And how many of them have left the church, but more important, the embrace of God, prematurely because they are disenchanted? No, to receive the gifts of being in communion with God, we must show patience, waiting for God while God waits for us.

Finally, complete surrender to God requires *trust*. God is Spirit, and that reality dumfounds many of us. We would really rather see to what or to whom we are giving ourselves, but we cannot. The irony is that we are not allowed to "see" God until we have walked with God for a while. By that time, we do not have the need to see; God's wonder and power have been shown to us, and we are content. But as we grow comfortable with God's presence and work, God begins to reveal the Divine Self to us. God comes in all ways, through people and situations, and only our trust in God's presence makes us know that we have "seen" God. Before that ever happens, though, we have to trust that God loves us, that God has our best interests at heart, that God does not want us to suffer, that God hears our pain, that God will direct our paths to heights we cannot begin to imagine, that God has the whole world in the divine hands, even and especially us. We have to trust that wherever God leads us will be better than where we are right now. And we have to trust that God knows all the human time limits that are in place and that we are duty-bound, as temporal beings, to honor.

What does this complete surrender, defined and encapsulated by desire, patience, and trust, yield us? The ability not to worry when the world would say to go ahead and do it. This complete surrender allows us to march to the tune of a different drummer, to hear what others cannot hear or understand. It allows us to have the "peace which transcends all understanding" because God is truly "hiding us in the tabernacle" (Ps. 27:5, NIV).

Example? Well, I am divorced, and at the time of the divorce, I had two small children, ages two and four. In two years, we had moved three times. It was awful and slightly embarrassing as church members dutifully came to help me each time.

One day, I could hear God say, "Buy a house." How do I know it was God? Because once you have heard God, the voice is unmistakable. And I heard God say, "Buy a house." I was cynical and sarcastic: "And what, pray tell, am I supposed to do that with?" I had no money and no credit. That did not seem to matter to God. God continued to give me the message; reluctantly, I began the process.

I had no money for a down payment. I had never saved for a house; I had been too busy making ends meet. My pastor's salary was not nearly enough to even consider a house, not with the children, day care expenses, and daily living expenses. I had no spare time to get an extra job to earn more money. I repeated my question to God, "How am I supposed to do this?"

It was an example of hearing God say, "Be still, and know that I am God" (Ps. 46:10, NIV), and doing it. I actually felt led by God through the process. Sometimes, I would be riding in my car, and I would think about what I was doing and a wave of anxiety would flood over me. Then I would hear God say, "No! Don't do that! I've got this one." And I would relax.

One day, the realtor called and wanted to show me several houses. When he took me into the third house, I knew which one I wanted. I had the audacity to say I wanted it, as if I had the resources. In fact, I had a tussle with God as I said it because I just knew that whatever had to "go through" would not and I would look stupid. That wave of anxiety came again, and I could hear God say, "Uh-uh. Let go!" And I did.

It seems that when God wants to show divine glory, God can do whatever God wants. In this case, I wanted to buy a house, and I didn't even have the money for a down payment. But God put me in touch with people I would never have known to talk to. And they began to teach me and show me the ways this "impossibility" could be made a reality. So I began to look at houses. I would have looked for something far different from what I was advised I could afford, but I was shown that the monthly payment on a house I thought was out of my range was about what I was paying for my leased house and what I had paid as rent on an apartment! I was amazed, but it was as if God had the helm and was in control. It was as if God said, "My son fed the five thousand; don't you think we can do this for you?" Where I had been worried, I was put to peace. I bought an incredible house. It's beautiful. I can afford it. I make my payments on time. I pay no more as a home owner than I did as a renter—only now, I get benefits that I didn't have before. It's as if God wanted to reward me, to show me how magnificent faith can be. The "feeding of the five thousand" happened to me and for me!

It is true that God will keep those in perfect peace who trust in God. It is amazing that we can even think about doing what the Sermon on the Mount demands that we do: "Do not worry about your life, what you will eat or what you will drink, or about your body, what you will wear. . . . Can any of you by worrying add a single hour to your span of life?" (Matt. 6:25–27). Worry is the antithesis of faith. You cannot say you believe if you worry. Some way, in your deepest sorrow, at your gloomiest hour, you have to be able to say, "God has it!"

Now, you may balk at this idea. I have heard people say that such an attitude is not using what God gave us—that is, a brain. These people say that God would not have given us a brain if we were not supposed to use it.

But not using our brains is not the issue. Relying on faith as opposed to worrying means that we allow God to direct the paths that our brains and our spirits take. A worry-laden spirit is a paralyzed spirit; a faith-filled spirit is energized and anticipatory. A worry-laden spirit expects defeat, but a faith-filled spirit expects what eyes cannot see. A faith-filled spirit moves ahead on the energy provided by God and does not become discouraged to the point of inaction. It attempts to soar above adversity and hard times to find solutions because God is leading it that way, and in all cases it finds the solutions.

Now, is the solution what human beings might have expected? Not all the time. But it is a solution that only God could have produced, such as the peaceful spirit experienced by a young girl dying of bone cancer. The "saints" who prayed for her had decided that if she was not physically healed, then her faith was weak. God told her that in the midst of her illness, she could and would experience communion with God, and that was her healing. When she lost her anxiety, she gained her peace and suffered very little the last few days of her life. Before she slipped into unconsciousness, though, she let us know that God held her and God was healing her spirit. She was in perfect peace; she worried about nothing.

What does the Bible say about people who worry? Turn to Matthew 13. Contained in this chapter of the Gospel is the story of a farmer who sowed some seeds:

> As he sowed, some seeds fell on the path, and the birds came and ate them up. Other seeds fell on rocky ground, where they did not have much soil, and they sprang up quickly, since they had no depth of soil. But when the sun rose, they were scorched; and since they had no root, they withered away. Other seeds *fell among thorns, and the thorns grew up and choked them.* Other seeds fell on good soil and brought forth grain, some a hundredfold, some sixty, some thirty. Let anyone with ears listen! (Matt. 13:4–9; italics added)

The Word of God is the seed, and Jesus is asking us, "What kind of soil do you have within? What is your breeding ground like?" He explains that seed sown on your surface—the type of spirit that hears the Word emotionally and receives it quickly without going through the process of desire, patience, and trust—will be eaten away with its first brush with the powers and principalities that are ever ready to swoop you up.

If your soil—your spirit—limits the depths to which it allows God to enter, then the Word sown within you will sprout, but again, it will be challenged and will probably die off when the heat of life warms it up. In other words, when troubles come, when the usual challenges of life come, the Word sown in this kind of spirit will wither and die because there is no root.

For the purposes of this discussion on anxiety, we must pay attention to the seed sown in the midst of the thorns. Worry chokes us. We do not have enough money, and we wake up in the middle of the night. As we worry, we cannot function, cannot eat. When we think about our dilemma, we literally almost stop living. Jesus said that this is like "the worries of this life and the deceitfulness of wealth" (Matt. 13:22, NIV) and that these worries and the deceitfulness make us unfruitful. Remember, a worried spirit is paralyzed. You cannot take anything in or put anything out. You are in a state of nothingness and can bear no fruit. Not for yourself. Not for your family. And especially not for God.

What are you worried about?

- The rent/mortgage is due, and you are several months behind.
- You have been laid off, and there is no new job in sight.
- Try as hard as you might, you have not been able to reach your teen son.
- Graduation is coming up, and you don't have enough money to give your child what everybody else has.
- You interviewed for the job you have always wanted, but you're not sure how you did.
- You have a secret you should have divulged a long time ago; now you are afraid it will come out and you will lose all that is important to you.
- You have not been feeling well, and you are worried it is something serious.
- You are worried that your pastor will condemn you if you share something about your past.

I could go on. The effort you must make during this journey is to shake off the worry. You must believe in a new way that if you let go, God will catch you. You must believe that if you truly put this burden in God's hands, God will direct your path, and you will find a solution. It is a promise. No single problem was ever solved by and through worry; only through surrender to God and to divine direction were solutions found. You must go inside yourself now and find God; you must pray as you have never prayed before for God to release you from yourself so that you can be in divine care.

Your spirit will react to whatever you feed it. If you feed it worry, it will worry, but if you feed it faith, it will breathe faith, and you will soar. Your problems will not go away, but you will experience the power of the living God to solve them or to cope with them. It is part of what resurrection is all about. It is about getting up when the world thought it had nailed the coffin shut.

Now, what are you going to do? Continue to worry, and you will have no victory. You will not move a single step from where you are right now. Let go and try to move in faith, and see what happens. By the end of this journey, you will have released the cross and will be free. This spirit of worrying is a yoke of bondage; it is a manifestation of spiritual slavery. Jesus took his journey, and now you take yours so that the yoke will be forever abandoned. "It is for freedom that Christ has set us free. Stand firm, then, and do not let yourselves be burdened again with a yoke of slavery" (Gal. 5:1, NIV).

Devotion Direction

Read Psalm 39:6; Matthew 6:5–34; 13:3–23; Luke 10:41; 21:34; Philippians 4:6; and 1 Peter 5:7.

1. About what are you worried? Write it in your journal and explain *to yourself* why this situation or situations worry you so much.

2. Write a prayer explaining this situation to God.

3. List the things you have changed by worrying. By contrast, list the things that have changed as you have given them to God. If you do not think you have ever given any of your burdens to God, be honest about it and write it down.

4. Which of the scriptures listed above give you the most comfort? Why?

eight

Bent, Broken, and Besieged by Bitterness

The middle-aged woman, Gloria, sat stiffly in her pastor's office. She had made the appointment to talk with the pastor, but now that she was here, she was not so sure she had done the right thing.

She had come because she had been moved by a series of sermons her pastor had given on glitches of the spirit. These glitches got in the way of the gifts of the Spirit, and the woman found herself, maybe for the first time, wrestling with a feeling she had carried for a long, long time.

Years before, when she was young and it was easier, it seemed, to believe in a beneficent God, Gloria had given birth to a baby boy. From the moment he was born, he was special. His spirit could light up a room or cheer the most downcast mood. His laughter was contagious, and his ability to let that laughter peal at the most critical times was eerie sometimes in its timeliness.

Many times his mother looked at him in amazement, thanking God for this gift and asking God to protect him always. It seemed that she knew that with a child so special, he would not ever be hers alone, but in sharing him with the world, she wanted to know that God was protecting him. It was the best she could ask.

She had other children, and the family was close, but always, Jonathan, this firstborn son, stood out. She breathed sighs of relief as he passed first through preschool, then elementary and middle schools. She was beaming with pride and relief when at last the time was approaching for him to graduate from high school. He had survived football injuries, teenage parties, and the temptation to experiment with drugs and alcohol; she knew that because he had told her. Finally, she thought, she would be able to relax a bit. Maybe her prayers had been answered.

And then came that horrible night when he went out and did not come home on time. Instantly, she worried because it was not like him. Whenever he was going to be late, he would call her, and she would be relieved at hearing his reassuring voice on the other end of the phone, "Hi, Mom! Don't worry. I'm home sooner than you can worry some more!" She would fuss a little, but relax. Sure enough, he would turn up, give her a big kiss and hug, and things would be okay.

But this night was different. He was late, and there was no call. Despite her best efforts, she was worried. By morning, she was frantic. She waited the specified time to call the police to report her son as missing, but she was livid at having to wait. She had been out looking for him the night before but had had no luck. She was angry when the police gave her the standard answer: she had to wait before she reported him missing.

The police began their search, and for two days, three days, there was nothing to report. And then, on the fourth day, came the dreaded news. Could she please come downtown to identify a young man who had been found beaten to death? Not just beaten. Mutilated. He was not recognizable. Gloria took a deep breath and went with the police officers. She saw the remains of what had been her beautiful, wonderful son.

Through the trial she sat, glaring at the man who murdered her son. She wanted him to die; she wanted him to be hung by his fingernails and suffer—then die. She rejoiced when the jury found him guilty, but recoiled when they declared him guilty of second-degree rather than first-degree murder, because of a technicality. Well, even at that, the crime had been brutal, and surely, the judge would sentence him to life in prison without parole. But he did not. According to the law, he could not. The longest sentence the judge could impose was twenty-five years to life, with a chance of parole after fifteen years. Gloria was stunned.

That was twenty-five years ago, and still, it seemed, she was stunned. But it was more than that. She was bitter. Bitter because she felt the police had not done their job. Bitter because the law said a person had to be missing twenty-four hours before he or she could be considered missing. Bitter because the American judicial system allowed so many loopholes that made it possible for criminals to go free. And bitter because she felt God had betrayed her.

To be bitter is to have an anguished spirit, to be in pain that is worse than pain. Anguish is a feeling that cannot be assuaged. It throbs like a physical pain for which painkillers do nothing. It throbs, ebbs for a while, then comes back. It never allows you to feel really good. Underneath everything you do and say, underneath every smile, every gesture, is this anguish, pulsating, throbbing, reminding you of a hurt that will not go away.

It is worse than active anger because bitterness may be more easily disguised. So, a person "on the other end" may be able to say that you are acting the way you are because you are angry, but when you are bitter, the person on the other side does not know how to identify what is going on. He or she knows only that it is not pleasant to be in your company.

Bitterness sends off vibes that you cannot control. It is as though it builds an impenetrable wall between you and the rest of the world. The message is, "Nobody will ever hurt me again!" The wall assures not only that, but assures that no one will be able to really reach you. And the sad thing is that the wall often keeps God out as well.

The anguish does it. As I watched Fred Goldman, the father of Ron Goldman, after the O. J. Simpson murder trial, I felt his bitterness. He was (and is) an anguished father who could not believe what he had just witnessed, and I could see that his bitterness would be his obsession. O. J. Simpson would get what he deserved, according to Fred Goldman.

As I continue to watch, I see the bitterness continuing. It is not enough that the judgment was rendered in the civil trial against O. J.

Simpson. Goldman wants to see O. J. suffer. He wants O. J. to lose as much as he can, seeing that he, Fred Goldman, has lost so much. He wants O. J. to feel the anguish of loss and more. The bitterness is the driver.

This is not to say that I or anyone else in Goldman's situation would feel different. I do not know that I would be as obsessed with ruining another human being if a not guilty verdict had been given and it had been my child, but if I was as convinced as is Goldman that the acquitted person was guilty, I probably would devote my attention to making sure the world knew of his guilt, the double jeopardy provision of our legal system notwithstanding. But I have felt bitterness; I have felt the anguish of soul that makes me want to make sure someone who has hurt me hurts just as much.

I watched while the father of another murder victim spewed his bitterness at the convicted killer of his daughter. After years of incarceration, the man spoke of being born again and of wanting to preach the Word of God to others, to save them. The father was outraged, and his bitterness made him say, "Well, if God can use a person like that, I don't want any part of God!"

When my mother died, I was bitter toward God. All I felt I had was my mother, and for her to be taken from me when she was so young (forty-five) and I was so young (a teen) did something to me. I was angry at and bitter toward God. I was also angry at and bitter toward the doctors who had misdiagnosed her cancer of the ovaries. I was so bitter that for a long time, I would not go to church, and to this day, I pretty much stay away from doctors.

Bitterness clouds our vision and our thinking; it makes us carry distorted pictures of reality and makes us discard spirituality altogether. Any discussion of grace—how it is unmerited and goes to everyone the same—might make us angry. We scoff at God, the One who created us and who can wipe any pain away if we will let God. We turn up our noses at the thought of forgiveness, and we justify our unwillingness to do what God commands. The anguish within the bitterness turns us from who we are to creatures that we would not recognize if confronted with ourselves.

Why does the anguish come? At the moment our pain comes upon us, we turn away from God instead of toward God. Jesus, it seemed, was in anguish as he prayed in the Garden of Gethsemane and, for a moment, turned from God. "If there be any way this can be taken from me," he asked. But when he said, "Nevertheless, not my will, but thine be done," it seemed that he garnered strength from somewhere and the ability not to hate those who were betraying him and denying him and who did not even recognize him as he was led into his suffering. By ourselves, we cannot handle the megapains that come our way. God is there for us when those pains hit. When we do not seek God's help in those places, we become vulnerable and susceptible to all kinds of attacks upon the spirit. In our woundedness, we inhale and digest things that will not let us be cured of the pain. The pain stays inside, festers, spoils, and makes us bitter, unhappy people.

Why would we even be in a place where we would deny God? Because for too many of us, God exists to satisfy *us*. We are okay as long as we can tell God how we want our lives to be. When God does not comply with what we want, we get angry and turn from God. We use God when it is convenient; we do not take the time to build a relationship with God that can hold up when things do not go our way. We do not understand how this omnipotent, omniscient God, this all-loving, all-merciful God, could let certain things happen to us.

That is why we ask a question like this: "Why does God let bad things happen?" We do not realize that God is not a magician or a dictator. Surely, God could make everyone believe in God and do what God says. But what would that do to the free will God created in all of us? How would God know which people wanted salvation and which ones were saved only because it was part of life? Jesus said that if we wanted to be his disciples, we had to deny ourselves and follow him. That denial is a choice, and God wants us to choose the Divine One. If God gave us the Divine Self without our having to make a choice, we would not appreciate all the things God offers and all the rewards that come from choosing God after realizing that our way was not *the Way*.

"Yes," you ask, "but how about the disease and suffering and pain in the world? Why doesn't God take all that away?" Again, it would be interfering with the incredible brains God gave us to be cocreators in this universe. Because of our brains, we have invented vaccines and computers and ways to get to the moon. Our brains have moved God's creation to the magnificent production that it is now. But in that cocreativity, some bad choices have been made; some wrong roads have been chosen. In the grand scheme of things, God has decided to take the bitter with the sweet for the good of the whole.

But that explanation does not set well with you, does it? No, you hurt because God could have saved your daughter, your son, your spouse. I know. I felt that way, too, when my mother died. And God sat patiently and waited for me to come home, to receive the Divine Self into my self and to be made whole. It took a long, long time.

Now, I see people immersed in bitterness, and I whisper, "Please let it go." Bitter spirits rob them and the people around them of Jesus' joy, the joy that passes all understanding. What better witness to the strength, power, and majesty of God than to have gone through a hideous experience and emerged not bitter but able to forgive and show grace and mercy like God shows us! To be bitter is to be a tree that will not bear fruit of the Spirit—love, joy, peace, patience, kindness, goodness, faithfulness, gentleness, and self-control (Gal. 5:22–23). Bearing the fruit of the Spirit is a more powerful way to live than being steeped in bitterness. Unfortunately, the more bitterness you exude, the more of it you draw to yourself. So, already hampered by a "sick" spirit, you draw only more sickness to yourself.

How does it work? Bitterness comes out in your eyes, in your body language and movement, and in the way you handle everyday experiences. The salesclerk makes a mistake, and instead of giving her room to be human, you make a nasty scene; she reacts in kind; your sore, anguished spirit riles up and strikes out; and in the end, you have done things and said things that were completely uncalled for. In the same situation, a healed spirit responds to the salesclerk's mistake and maybe to her bitterness with kindness, and a completely different outcome is experienced. Where do you most often find yourself?

Consider the story of a bitter woman, Sarai, the wife of Abram, found in chapter 16 of the book of Genesis (NIV). She was advanced in years and had not been able to bear a child. From her comment, "the Lord has kept me from having children," we can see her bitterness. Bitter people often blame anyone, including God, for their feelings or for their lot in life.

She was bitter because in those times, a woman's worth was defined by her ability to bear children, especially sons. It did not matter how beautiful she was or how wealthy.

At her age, Sarai thought it was impossible to have any children. In order not to disappoint her husband, she suggested that he sleep with Hagar, her Egyptian maidservant.

Of all people. Her servant, a woman who was years younger than Sarai, beautiful, and able to bear children. Sarai fumed not only that God would keep her from having children, but also that God would put in her presence, and her husband's, a woman who would one-up her.

Abram agreed to sleep with her, and Hagar bore a son, Ishmael. Sarai's bitterness grew. When someone is bitter, her rationality decreases; she cannot see straight or think as she usually would because her bitterness drives her. Sarai had told Abram to sleep with Hagar; Hagar had not suggested it. But because she was an anguished spirit, Sarai began to transfer that anguish outwardly and began to blame Abram for her pain. She was so angry, so hurt, so bitter, that she uttered a curse upon her husband, "May God judge between you and me!" (Gen. 16:5).

Abram at that point put Hagar in Sarai's hands and told her to do with the young woman whatever she wanted, and Sarai "mistreated Hagar so that she fled from her" (Gen. 16:6).

It does not say so in the Scriptures, but surely, in her quiet moments, when the bitterness was given time to rest, Sarai was surprised and repulsed by her actions. But like one addicted to a substance over which she has no control, Sarai had no control. When she "awoke" from those moments, moments when she remembered how she used to be or how she used to act, she descended once again to the depths to which bitterness had pulled her.

Does that sound familiar? In your bitterness, have you said things, done things, that you wish you had not said or done? Do you sometimes want to cry out, after you have acted unkindly, that you are not really that way?

More important, can you feel right now the anguish that has been driving you and making you bitter for so long? Being bitter is not going to cure you. If in your bitterness, you make the person who hurt you hurt as well, you will not feel better. No, you have to be willing to relinquish the bitterness and give it to God. Let God replace it with something that will work for you.

That something is forgiveness. You will never be free until you let go and forgive. Whatever happened, it is over. But you are still in prison. You are miserable and unable to feel the power of God. I remember how liberating it was to finally stop being bitter toward my ex-husband. It did not happen overnight, but I was amazed at how free I felt once I let go. Because of the kind of person I am, I have to go through many struggles like that. Yet it never fails; every time I let go, I feel freer.

To be healed of this bitterness, to be relieved of this burden on this journey, you have to agree to stop today giving your bitterness its power, which is your spirit. That person on whom you have devoted so many hours of bitter, mean, vengeful thoughts is not the one on whom you should concentrate any more effort. Concentrate on the One with whom you are carrying a cross right now. Your bitterness is your cross, and you are on this journey to lay down the cross. Name the person or persons. By name, say who they are and say why you are so bitter. And then ask God to show you how to pray in order to get to the place where you can pray in the spirit of forgiveness and mercy.

A footnote: the woman in the scenario at the beginning of this chapter does not really exist, but I can tell of the liberation I have seen in several cases like hers, where the family of the victim has decided to forgive. I have seen the liberation in South Africans I have met who, instead of remaining bitter about the reality and the brutality of apartheid, have decided to let go and be free. I have noticed the liberation of some African Americans in this country who, in deciding to let go of bitterness and to hold on to the American Dream as best they could, reaped more rewards than those who remained—and remain—bitter. I have seen women who were raped and remained bitter, never having a good relationship with a man their whole lives, and I have seen women who were raped and let go of the bitterness, living wonderful, productive lives. Being bitter, or remaining bitter, makes you a victim. Letting go of the bitterness makes you a victor! You are on your way to victory, to get out of the prison in which sits a sick spirit. By the end of this journey, you should be able to say, "Free at last! Free at last! Thank God Almighty, I'm free at last!"

Devotion Direction

Read Genesis 16–17 and Luke 22:54–71.

1. Examine Sarai's bitterness. Did Hagar have any reason to be bitter as well? How did their bitterness affect them?

2. Why does God let bad things happen? As you look now on the things that have happened that have made you bitter, can you see any reason why God might have allowed those things to happen? What were you supposed to learn or share from your experiences?

3. What other biblical figures showed bitterness? Why? What happened to them? Did they hold on to the bitterness or let go of it?

4. To let go of your bitterness, you have to identify it and pray about it. Are you willing to take this intimate journey with God?

5. If God told you to go to the person against whom you hold this pain, what would you do? Would you be able to obey?

Prayers and Exercises for the Journey

LETTING GO OF THE ANGER

Prayer

God, for too long, I have been angry. I have held it in and pretended that it was not important, but it is. I know, merciful God, that you have shown me mercy, and that you have forgiven me countless times. And I know that I'm supposed to forgive myself and others. But I haven't and I haven't really even wanted to try. I can't understand why this had to happen. I don't want to try to understand. I'm too angry, and I know that this anger is eating me up. Worse than that, O God, it is keeping me from communion and relationship with you.

Help me, God. I give myself and this anger to you. Open my ears so that I can hear your voice, and then give me the strength to do what you would have me do. I know the Word says that if others offend us, we're supposed to go to them before we lay our gifts to you on the altar. Today, I can't do that, but if I have to do that in order to do your will, then please, give me the strength.

I give myself and this anger to you this day, O God.

Exercises

To be healed, I must reveal the problem and the situation to myself.

My anger is or has been directed toward

_____

because (write down the situation)

_____

_____

_____

This (situation, person) made me angry because

_____

_____

_____

When I think about this (situation, person), I want to

_____

_____

_____

I would feel better if _____

_____

_____

_____

My goal is to ___ go to the person or ___ call the person and be honest about this by

_____ (date).

I need God to help me do the following:

_____

_____

_____

AN UNFORGIVING SPIRIT

Prayer

Most loving God, I confess to you that I hold an unforgiving spirit. I confess that instead of wanting to show forgiveness as you have shown me, I want the persons who hurt me so badly to hurt as they hurt me. I confess that although I haven't actively done anything to hurt them, I want something "just" to happen to them. I want to see them hurt. I confess that when I heard that they had fallen on bad times, I rejoiced. In fact, I hope bad things will happen to them because I think they deserve bad things.

I know I am forgetting how many times I have hurt you, O loving God. I know I am forgetting that if you didn't forgive, I wouldn't be here right now. I know that I have hurt you again and again and not even known it, and I know that in spite of that, you have forgiven me again and again.

Loving God, help me let go of this spirit of vengeance and accusation. Help me to see you in what I do and say. Help me remember that I am called to be the salt of the earth and, in so doing, be an example of how you'd want us to act. I can't forgive these people on my own, God. I need you. Please, hear my prayer.

I give myself and this unforgiving spirit to you today, O God.

Exercises

To be healed, I must reveal the problem and the situation to myself.

I hold an unforgiving spirit against _____ .

I have held this unforgiving spirit since _____ .

The situation that brought this about in me was _____

_____

_____

_____

_____

It has been hard for me to forget and forgive the situation or person because

---

When I think of the situation or person, some of my reactions include the following:

Pray Psalm 51:10 daily:

"Create in me a clean heart, O God, and put a new and right spirit within me."

"Create in me a pure heart, O God, and renew a steadfast spirit within me" (NIV).

To be healed of this unforgiving spirit, I think I must

LET GO OF THE FEAR!

Prayer

I know, O God, that fear and faith cannot exist in the same space. I know that if I believe in you and I love you, I shouldn't be afraid. But I am. I am afraid to trust you, and that's why I'm afraid of (name your cross). I don't want to be afraid anymore. I want to be free. I want to know what it is like to feel you beneath my spirit, taking me way over the things that have me captive right now. I know that to fear you is to doubt you, and that to do that is a sin, but by myself, I seem helpless to let go.

Loving God, hear me. Hear my pleading and my desperation. I don't want to be this way anymore. Please, God, show me what I have to do. I am willing to listen to you now in ways I was never willing to before. I don't want life to pass me by with this fear still in my spiritual space. I know that you came so that we could be free, so I am asking for you to give me your Holy Spirit, to beat away the powers and principalities that have me captive. I don't promise that I'll be able to do immediately what you tell me, but I am willing to do whatever I have to do to reach the point that I have the strength to obey.

Please, hear my prayer, O God.

Exercises

To be healed, I must reveal the problem and the situation to myself.

I am afraid of _____

_____

_____

(Examples might include fear of heights, the dark, or tunnels; fear of trusting anyone at all; fear of trusting the opposite sex; fear of commitment; fear of flying; fear of telling the truth. Be deliberate and honest in your self-examination.)

I have had this fear since _____ .

The situation that made me realize this fear, or the situation that produced this fear, was

_____

_____

_____

Read Matthew 14:22–31. Peter began to sink when he

_____

Can you see in this passage how fear hampers your spiritual fullness? Explain:

_____

_____

_____

To let go of this fear, I have to

_____

_____

_____

WHEN THERE IS NOT ENOUGH FAITH

Prayer

Loving Father, I stretch my hands to you. Loving Mother, I reach for you. I cannot find you in the way that I need, and I confess that it has made me inherit a spirit of faithlessness.

I listen to all these people talk about God and about how you do so many things for them, but when I look at my life, I cannot see the same things. I don't know why you seem to talk to some of your children, but not to others. I certainly don't hear you talk to me. I wonder why everybody else seems to talk about miracles you perform, and yet when I look around, I cannot see or sense the same things.

When I needed you most, you didn't come through, and that has bothered me. I don't know how to talk to you or how to understand how you work. I know only that I had always heard that if we knocked, you'd answer the door, but when I knocked, you didn't come.

What am I doing wrong, O God, and what do I need to do differently? How should I pray in order to hear you? What should I do in order to see you? Why do so many other people seem to have so much joy and have so much connectedness to you when I do not and cannot seem to get there?

Hear me, O God. I am on this journey because I want to drop this spirit of unfaithfulness. I need you as I have never needed you before. I am willing, O God, to do what you tell me. Please, hear my prayer.

Exercises

To heal, I must confess and reveal the problem to myself.

I do not believe in God the way that I want to because

_____

_____

_____

I have never believed in God or I stopped believing in God because

_____

_____

_____

Getting more faith is important now for me because

_____

_____

_____

Read Mark 9:14–32. Concentrate on verse 24:

"I do believe; help me overcome my unbelief!" (NIV).

About what situation in your life would you have to give an answer like this one?

_____

_____

_____

How do you think God would respond to you?

_____

_____

_____

Why do you feel that way?

_____

_____

_____

When you read the story of the casting out of the evil spirit, what did you think?

_____

_____

_____

List the things about which you have serious doubt:

_____

_____

_____

Write a prayer asking God to help you with your area (or areas) of disbelief:

_____

_____

_____

_____

_____

SHAKING LOOSE OF THE GREEN-EYED MONSTER

Prayer

Dear God, I don't want to be this way anymore.

I know that I have a lot to be grateful for. I know that I am special in your eyes. And yet I am jealous. I am jealous of (name your situation), and I hate it. Sometimes it scares me because in my jealousy, I sometimes feel rage. I feel that I could do something really bad or say something bad. I feel out of control. There really isn't any reason for me to feel this way, and yet I do. I need your help.

What is broken within me, O God, that makes me see the worst in every situation or person? What in me won't I trust so that I cannot trust anyone else? What have I done to make me think that other people have dishonorable intentions against me? Am I afraid that what I have done or thought about will come back to haunt me? Will it?

I know that if I cannot trust myself or others, it means I don't trust you, and I don't want that. I can't have peace like this, O God. Please, hear my prayer. Give me the way to liberation from this jealousy that is ruining my spirit and my life. Hear me, O God.

Exercises
To heal, I must confess and reveal the problem to myself.

I am jealous of _____ .

I have felt this jealousy for _____ (how long).

I have always been jealous ___ / only recently noticed it ___ .

What makes you jealous?_____

_____

_____

If your husband or wife (or boyfriend or girlfriend) makes you jealous, what causes your jealousy? Be very specific.

_____

_____

_____

Looking at the responses you just wrote, do you believe that your feelings are justified or that they represent something askew in you? Why?

_____

_____

_____

Complete this sentence: I'm a jealous person because

_____

_____

Read 1 Samuel 18. How did Saul's jealousy affect his personality?

_____

_____

_____

How does your jealousy affect your personality and your behavior?

_____

_____

_____

Write a prayer. Prayer is not just petition; it is confession, praise, and thanksgiving as well. To be healed, you have to confess, then ask God for what you need. When your healing comes, you can then write a prayer of thanksgiving and praise. Write a prayer here explaining to God why you are jealous and when jealousy rears its ugly head. Be specific.

_____

_____

_____

_____

Now, write a prayer asking (petitioning) God for what you need in order to have victory over your jealousy.

_____

_____

_____

_____

_____

BE ANXIOUS FOR NOTHING

Prayer
Dear God, hear me.

I know that I am not supposed to worry about things, not since I believe in you. I know that you tell us not to worry about what we shall eat or drink, or what we shall wear, because you know our needs and you won't let us suffer. I know that you are a miracle-making God, but in my situation, God, I haven't been able to let go of my anxiety over (name your situation).

_____

Even as I pray this, there is a gnawing in the back of my mind. It's as if the worry won't let go of me! I try to shake it loose, but it holds on and affects my thoughts. You've never deserted me. I have had bad times, sure, but when I look back, I can see you. In retrospect, even if I couldn't recognize your presence at the time, I know you have always been with me and have always taken care of me.

So why do I keep worrying? God, I want to have a new life, a new way of looking at things. You are my light and my life, and I want to really live that way, not always looking back over my shoulder. I know that in doing that, I give evil power over me, I want you to teach me how to "let go and let God." I don't know how to do that. I don't know how to just let you handle my life.

This day, O God, begin working in me as you never have before, to cut away the parts of me that continue to hold on to worry and to replace the parts with a spirit of trust in you.

Exercises
To be healed, I must confess and reveal the situation to myself.

I worry about _____

I worry for these reasons: _____

_____

_____

_____

I haven't given this situation (or situations) to God because (check one)

___ I don't know how.

___ I don't want to.

___ I don't believe God can handle it.

Read Matthew 6:25–34.
When I read this, I think Jesus is saying:

_____

_____

_____

Why do you think Jesus admonishes us not to worry?

_____

_____

_____

In the Bible, worry is actually forbidden. Read the following scriptures, and find one or two on which you can meditate: Psalm 127:2; Luke 10:41; 12:11–12; 12:20; 12:25–26; 21:34; Philippians 4:6; 1 Corinthians 7:32; and 1 Peter 5:7.

Write about your understanding of the statement "Let go and let God":

_____

_____

_____

_____

_____

BENT, BROKEN, AND BESIEGED BY BITTERNESS

Prayer

Hear my prayer, O God.

Inside me, where there should be at least space for the influx of your blessed Holy Spirit, I have an ugliness that swirls and churns and ever reminds me of its presence.

I am a bitter person, God, and I hate it.

I have tried to shake it, but I haven't had much luck. Every time I think of (name your situation),

_____

I can feel those awful feelings rising up again. And because of those feelings, I feel bad inside.

My bitterness consumes me. I know because even though my situation happened a long time ago, the *feelings are as raw as though the situation happened just yesterday.* I say confession at the beginning of every month, before I take communion, but I confess today that I haven't ever really confessed these feelings. I have kept them intensely personal and hidden and guarded.

I know it's displeasing to you. I know that we are called to let go of the poisons in our spirits, but without your help, I cannot. Please, hear me, O God. If ever I needed you, it is now.

Exercises

To be healed, I must confess and reveal the situation to myself.

I am bitter about

_____

I have been carrying this "cross" for

_____ (period of time).

This situation has made me bitter because

_____

_____

_____

_____

Read Lamentations 3. The writer is bitter. Describe his feelings. Is his bitterness directed toward God, human beings, or both? How does it make him sound?

_____

_____

_____

_____

_____

Can you see or identify any of yourself or your feelings in what this writer gives us? Describe.

_____

_____

_____

_____

_____

One of the best ways to get rid of a negative feeling or emotion is to identify a few positive ones that can be juxtaposed against the negative. Does the writer do this? In which verses?

_____

_____

_____

_____

What are some positive emotions you can identify, even about the situation that has made you so bitter, that may be able to help you move from your cross to victory?

_____

_____

_____

_____

_____

As you identify and dissect the thing or things that have made you so bitter, meditate each day on the positives so that you can name the "new mercies" that God has given you in spite of your other situation.

_____

_____

_____

_____

_____

REFLECTIONS